IT'S TIME TO
SPILL

the

BEANS

IT'S TIME TO SPILL
SPILL

the

BEANS

A Story of Greed

DAVID KLEIN

Table of Contents

Dear Reader,

My name is David Klein, the inventor of Jelly Belly jelly beans. In 1976, with only $800, I set out to create a jelly bean that would stand apart, each one packed with natural fruit purees and real flavors whenever possible, crafted with a passion for quality. And it worked. Jelly Belly became a sensation.

But in 1980, everything changed. Herm Rowland from the Herman Goelitz Candy Company forced my hand, and I had to sell the brand I had poured my heart and soul into. That moment marked a new chapter. I stayed involved in the candy business, constantly working on new ideas – but I wasn't allowed to compete with the jelly bean that had once been mine because of a 20 year non-compete clause. Over time, Herm began manipulating situations that only served to hurt me. Eventually, this led to a series of legal battles and, finally, a judgement that left me owing over $276,000 to the Jelly Belly Candy Company.

This book is my story – a memoir that begins with my childhood at age five and takes you through the ups and downs of a lifetime spent in the candy world. It's filled with stories, laughter, and lessons learned from my life, family, and the sweet, quirky world I've poured my life into.

My goal in sharing this isn't just to look back, but to invite you to understand the whole story, especially how I found myself in a position where my own creation was taken from me. Now, in my late 70s, it's a matter of principle. I don't want Herm or The Jelly Belly Candy Company to continue to financially control my future after they've already done enough to ruin me. Perhaps you, too, have faced situations where you were treated unfairly, where something you worked so hard to build was taken from your hands.

While I did go in front of a judge I never truly had the opportunity to fully present my case, So now I'm hoping that you, the reader, can help me take a stand against the wrongs that were done to me. Money might be able to buy a lot, but when friends and supporters share a message, it can be as powerful as the roar of a lion – reaching more people than I ever could alone. With your help, this book's story can reach far and wide, giving a voice to a deep injustice that needs to be heard.

Thank you for picking up this book. I appreciate you taking the time to read, to share, and to join me in this journey through a lifetime of candy and creativity.

With gratitude,

David Klein

Everything I Learned in Life,
I Learned Working in a Liquor Store

David Klein's first job came at an age when most children were just learning to tie their shoes. He wasn't even 6 years old when he began working at *The Lazy Bee*, the liquor store his grandparents and Aunt Ida owned in Van Nuys, California. By the time he turned 7, the store had already become the foundation of his young life, offering lessons in business, human nature, and the subtle art of entrepreneurship.

The Lazy Bee was more than just a place of commerce. It was a community hub, a gathering place where the smell of roasted nuts mingled with the buzz of conversation from locals who stopped by not just to shop, but to share stories and connect. For David, this store was where his love of business took root, growing in ways he couldn't yet understand.

His earliest memories are of sitting behind the cash register—a grand, gold-plated National Cash Register—watching the ebb and flow of customers. He would read the backs of candy bar wrappers, memorize the names of candy manufacturers, and learn where each product was made. "By the time I was 13, I could name every candy's origin," David would later recall, "I'd quiz my classmates, and when the teacher left the room, I'd lead a discussion: 'Name a candy bar.'" That simple game, a sign of his growing passion for candy, hinted at what was to come.

In those early years, Aunt Ida was a towering figure in his life—though not in stature. At just 4 feet 6 inches, she was known affectionately as *Shorty*, and she had a big personality to match. Ida, who could out-swear anyone but had the kindest heart, was David's guide into the world of retail. She taught him how to stock shelves, greet customers, and manage the store's inventory. Every week, she would take him to *Smart & Final*, the local wholesale store, where they'd select new candies to sell. David was always thrilled by these trips, excited to explore the latest offerings and help Aunt Ida choose the perfect mix for the store.

Back then, candy bars sold for 5 cents each, and a box of 24 bars would cost 80 cents wholesale. Shrink wrap didn't exist in those days. "If a customer wanted to try a candy bar," David explained, "they'd put a nickel in the box and take one out. That way, the store had already made a sale." These little quirks of the trade stuck with David, providing valuable insights into how business worked. It wasn't just about the product—it was about understanding people, anticipating their needs, and building a relationship with them.

And David certainly got to know the people who came through *The Lazy Bee*. There was Blossom, a regular customer with a massive St. Bernard dog, who gave David a rare 1909 SVDB penny on his seventh birthday. "Save this for a rainy day," she told him, "it'll be worth something someday." Sure enough, when David needed money for college, he sold the penny for $500—a small fortune at the time. Blossom's gift was more than just a coin; it was a reminder that even the smallest acts of kindness could leave a lasting impact.

The liquor store, however, wasn't just about candy and pennies. It was David's first introduction to the world of nuts—cashews and pistachios, in particular. He tasted his first cashew at the store, from a Fritos package that sold for 10 cents. Fritos also sold pistachios, which in those days were mostly dyed red to hide any blemishes. "No one really thought about why pistachios were red," David recalled, "but it was a clever way to make imperfect nuts more appealing." These early experiences with nuts would later inspire him to explore the nut business, adding yet another dimension to his entrepreneurial ambitions.

In addition to stocking candy and tasting nuts, David was responsible for helping with the store's cooler, where beer and soda were kept at a frosty 36 degrees. "I was just 7 years old, bundling up in a coat to stock the shelves," he laughed, remembering the chill of those cold boxes. The soda bottles had to be carefully organized, with a 2-cent deposit for returns. He still remembers the day the 7-Up driver, who had a cold box on his truck, handed him a couple of icy bottles as a sample. "It was the best taste on a hot summer day," David said, smiling at the memory, "and I can still recall it vividly, even after all these years."

One of the more extraordinary aspects of working at *The Lazy Bee* was the proximity to Hollywood. Van Nuys, located near Burbank, was home to many actors and actresses, and David's interactions with them became part of the fabric of his childhood. He attended school with Tony Dow, the actor who played Wally on *Leave It to Beaver*, and Mickey Dolenz, who would later become a member of *The Monkees*. David even delivered alcohol to Judy Garland's mother. "I'd walk to her house on Kester Avenue and leave the bottles in the garage, just like she asked," he said, recounting his childhood brush with fame.

But the store wasn't all glamour. David learned the nuts and bolts of running a small business—literally. He sorted comic books, arranged the soda shelves, and even learned how to detect counterfeit bills. "You didn't just greet a customer, you made them feel at home," he explained. "I'd carry out any large packages without asking, because that's just what you did." Through it all, David developed a work ethic and business acumen that would serve him well throughout his life.

David worked at *The Lazy Bee* from morning until night during the summer months, and after school and on weekends during the school year. He loved the rhythm of the store, the predictability of opening and closing, and the satisfaction of learning how things worked. "I never broke a bottle in all those years," David said proudly, reflecting on his young career as a stock boy and budding businessman.

David had a lot of time to teach himself more than just things about the candy industry. He enjoyed being unique and finding ways to set himself apart from others in even the simplest ways. He would spend many hours in the liquor store trying to catch flies with his bare hands till one day he figured out just the right move to do it. He's kept that talent all these years. Something else David does is to use paper plates to take his notes. He feels they stack nicely unlike sheets of paper in a pile.

The years rolled by, and David's connection to *The Lazy Bee* deepened. But as time went on, change was inevitable. The store eventually passed into new hands, and it was under new ownership when tragedy struck. A former owner named Abe, who had been a kind and hardworking man, was asked by the new owner to cover a Saturday shift. Abe agreed, but that afternoon, a man rode up to the store on a bicycle and shot him. The senseless act of violence sent shockwaves through the community, and David, now older, was deeply affected by the loss.

Looking back on those early years, David often said that everything he learned in life, he learned working in that liquor store. It wasn't just the skills he developed—stocking shelves, handling cash, dealing with customers—but the sense of connection he built with the people around him. From Aunt Ida's tough love and business savvy to Blossom's kindness and Abe's work ethic, *The Lazy Bee* shaped David into the man he would become.

For David, the store was a place of learning, of growth, and of inspiration. It was where his passion for candy and business was born, and where his future in the candy industry began to take shape. As he would often say in later years, "I didn't just learn how to sell candy. I learned how to be in the world."

It's Time to Make the Pizza

David could hardly contain his excitement when he landed his first official job at Luigi's Pizza, a bustling pizzeria on Victory Boulevard in North Hollywood.

The timing couldn't have been better. The job lined up just after his family had taken a short trip to Santa Barbara—a rare getaway they'd all been looking forward to. They stayed in one of the very first Motel 6's in the country, something David thought was pretty cool. Back then, it was called Motel 6 because the rooms were a mere six dollars a night. The motel sat conveniently across from a seafood restaurant, where they enjoyed some of the best BBQ David had ever tasted. But as luck would have it, David's job at Luigi's demanded his attention, and they had to cut the trip short so he could start on time.

David was due at Luigi's by 5 p.m. on Monday, so his mom drove him there since he was only fourteen and still couldn't get his driver's license. He did, however, have a work permit issued by his school, signed by his parents, which made him feel quite grown-up. When they arrived, Luigi himself, an older man with a gruff but lively demeanor, greeted David at the door.

"You look like you're ready to work," Luigi said, sizing him up with a squint in his eye, as if assessing whether this teenager had what it took to work in a busy pizza joint.

David felt the nervous excitement bubble up as he replied, "Where do I start?"

He had envisioned diving right into the pizza-making process, maybe even trying his hand at tossing the crust in the air like he'd seen in movies. When Luigi gestured to the broom instead, David's shoulders slumped for a moment, but he quickly put on a smile and got to work sweeping the floor.

Luigi wasn't just assigning tasks; he was watching David closely. After about twenty minutes, Luigi called David into his office. David wasn't sure what to expect—a pep talk? More instructions? But Luigi looked serious, leaning forward in his chair with his hands clasped in front of him.

"I've been watching you," he started, and David's heart raced, unsure if this was good or bad.

Luigi continued, "The dumbest people in the world are hired to sweep floors. I can tell you're not dumb, but you're never going to make it in this business. You're not coordinated enough to sweep with a broom."

David's stomach dropped. It was the last thing he'd expected to hear, and he felt a pang of disappointment and embarrassment.

"I'm going to have to let you go," Luigi said simply. He reached into his pocket and handed David a few coins for his one hour of work.

It was a quiet walk to the front counter, where Luigi handed him the phone. "Here," he said. "Use the phone so someone can pick you up."

David swallowed hard, fighting the lump in his throat. He dialed home, and when his mom answered, he tried to keep his voice steady.

"Can you please pick me up?" he asked.

There was a pause on the other end. "Are you alright?" she asked, sounding concerned. After all, he'd only been there an hour.

"Yeah," David said. "I'll explain when you get here." Luigi was hovering nearby, listening, so David kept it brief.

The car ride home was tense. David's mom knew something was wrong, but she waited for him to explain on his own terms. When they got home, he recounted the story to both his mom and dad, who listened in silence.

The next morning, however, his dad was anything but silent. All week long, David heard about how they'd cut their vacation short just so he could start his job at Luigi's, only to get fired after one measly hour. His dad seemed to grow more frustrated with each retelling, reminding David of the trip they'd sacrificed, the six-dollar motel, and the amazing seafood they'd missed out on just for this fleeting job.

Then, something unexpected happened.

On the very next day, David overheard his dad on the phone. "Yes, that's right," he was saying. "Six pizzas with pepperoni, anchovies, pineapple, jalapeños, sausage, and olives." David raised an eyebrow. That was quite the combination. "Could you please deliver them to 1245 Elm Street? Perfect, thank you!"

When his dad hung up, David asked, "Who was that?"

His dad glanced over with a shrug. "Just placing an order."

David paused, his mind catching up as he realized that 1245 Elm Street wasn't a real address.

In the end, that one night at Luigi's didn't quite turn out as David had imagined. But as he looked back, he'd always remember it as the night he took a first step out into the working world, learning lessons that went well beyond pizza-making.

Trying to Do Your Best

David's next adventure in the business world after Luigi's led him to managing a small, one-person steak house—so small, in fact, that there was no room for dining inside. A few bar stools lined the front, and two picnic tables with umbrellas offered seating for customers on the patio. The Steak Hut, which specialized in a Philly-style steak, was wedged between the bustling Encino Car Wash and Du-Par's, the legendary LA diner known for its iconic locations in Farmer's Market, Encino, and Studio City.

As David worked long days at The Steak Hut, he often thought about the men working hard across the lot at the car wash. He felt a deep sympathy for them, especially on rainy days when they'd be sent home without pay. Tips made up most of their income, so rainy days left them without much to take home.

Every Sunday, David would walk across the street to Du-Par's, dipping into the previous day's cash register to buy a dozen of the finest donuts, glossy and fresh, to sell at The Steak Hut. They were always a hit with his customers, adding a touch of sweetness to the simple menu.

David chuckled every time he thought of Mrs. Blankenship, the owner of The Steak Hut. She had a particular way of managing her business, even if it puzzled him at times. One day, David watched as Mrs. Blankenship approached a customer eating at one of the picnic tables. She peered at his plate and, pointing, asked, "Are you going to eat those pickles?" David couldn't make sense of it—did she want to eat them herself, or was she considering reusing them for another customer? The odd interaction stayed with him for over six decades, still bringing a smile to his face whenever he remembered it.

One night, Mrs. Blankenship called David at home, panicked. The previous day's cash bag was missing. David's mom quickly drove him to The Steak Hut, where he discovered another employee had stashed the bag in the wrong hiding spot. Relief washed over him, though he wondered why Mrs. Blankenship hadn't thought to look there herself.

Another day, a customer came by in the early morning for coffee. David handed him a steaming cup, but the man looked at it, puzzled, and said, "My cup is bleeding."

Confused, David looked closer and saw lipstick smudged on the ceramic rim. Mortified, he offered to replace the coffee, but the customer declined, leaving David red-faced and with a new level of vigilance for cleaning dishes.

One morning, a man from Detroit, Michigan, visited the stand, explaining that he'd just driven across the country to find Annette Funicello for an interview. David was taken aback by the man's determination and shared that he actually knew Annette's father, who owned the nearby Union 76 gas station. With directions in hand, the man went on his way, grateful and full of hope.

Around this time, David had a strange and unsettling experience with his dad. One evening, he had just returned home from a walk when, as he opened the back door, a window cracked and broke suddenly. His dad, who normally was the gentlest man David had ever known, heard the noise from another room, and his reaction was startling. Panicking, he grabbed a gun from the freezer—where David's mom kept it hidden—and came after David, mistaking him for a threat. David's dad chased him around the block, gun in hand, in a moment that felt more like a surreal dream than reality. David figured later that this incident must have been the result of some medication his father was taking, as it was so unlike him. They never spoke about it again.

One Sunday after work, David grew anxious, fearing he'd left The Steak Hut's gas on. He asked his dad if they could go back to check. Without hesitation, his dad agreed, despite it being his only day off. Once they arrived, David's suspicions were confirmed—the gas was indeed on. Just then, a customer pulled up, asking if The Steak Hut was open. "Sure, what do you need?" David replied, eager to make a sale and impress Mrs. Blankenship. After handing the man his $10 order—a sizable sale back then—David glanced outside just in time to see his dad abruptly pull away from the curb, leaving him there.

David took care of everything, turning the gas off and muttering, "Gas off," a habit he would carry with him for the rest of his life. Without a phone at The Steak Hut, he dug a dime out of his pocket and walked to the nearest payphone. When his dad picked up, David asked how he was supposed to get home, reminding him they were miles away. His dad's curt reply: "Walk, you S.O.B." Overhearing the conversation, David's mom quickly stepped in, coming to his rescue. "Thank you, Mom!" David would often think to himself, with deep gratitude.

After nearly a year at The Steak Hut, David felt it was time for a new direction. His paths would cross with Mrs. Blankenship one more time, years later, when a Los Angeles Times article about his invention, Jelly Belly, was syndicated by the Associated

Press. Mrs. Blankenship reached out, offering her best wishes: "It looks like you've come a long way from The Steak Hut. I wish you nothing but well."

For David, The Steak Hut had been more than a job—it was an unforgettable experience filled with quirky characters, hard lessons, and moments that would stay with him forever.

Sweet and Innocent

David's next job would leave a lasting mark. His Uncle Marty ran a custom tailor shop in Canoga Park, right next to a health food store owned by Johnny Weissmuller, the Olympic swimmer famed for playing Tarzan in the movies. Johnny was something of a local icon, known not just for his movie roles but as one of the first health food pioneers in the area. The neighborhood had a unique charm, shaped by its blend of glamour and wellness.

Just ninety yards behind Marty's shop was a small restaurant that became part of David's daily routine. Nearly every day, Marty would call out, "Dave, can you get me an egg sandwich and tell them it's for me—they know how I like it." It was always the same line, and David faithfully followed, ordering just as instructed. One afternoon, though, Marty forgot to pay him back for the sandwich. David, a bit shy back then, let it slide and kept on working.

Marty's shop was far from an ordinary tailor shop. He crafted custom suits for a range of clients, from Hollywood stars to employees at Rocketdyne, a prominent aerospace company. David admired the skill and care Marty poured into each suit, paying attention to every detail, from the precise measurements to the choice of fabric. His job was to help clients choose from various materials, with sharkskin being a popular choice at the time. David enjoyed describing its sleek look and feel, making customers feel they were getting something truly special.

One day, while tidying up the shop, David stumbled upon something unexpected in Marty's closet—a nudist magazine. Back then, these magazines were restricted to those over twenty-one, and David knew he was too young. But curiosity got the better of him, and he took a quick peek. That's when Marty spotted him and quickly called out, "Put that down! You're too young for that." David felt a wave of embarrassment and never forgot that moment.

David's other task was helping their tailor, Lupe, get home to Echo Park whenever he missed the bus—a frequent occurrence. David didn't mind; it was just another part of his routine.

Marty had his own way of doing things, even when it came to cleaning. "Never sweep the dirt toward a customer," he'd remind David, with a serious look. Over time, David improved in all aspects of the job—sweeping, showing fabrics, and learning the rhythms of the shop.

Eventually, David realized he had learned all he could from the job. Those days of egg sandwiches, sweeping, and quiet rides to Echo Park with Lupe taught him more than just tailoring. It was an experience he'd carry forward, one that left him with new skills, stories, and maybe even a few quirks of his own.

Big Dave's Popcorn

It was around this time that David's Uncle Earl asked if he wanted to come work with him. In David's documentary, viewers catch a glimpse of a popcorn factory—a place still standing today—which marks the exact location where Uncle Earl once crafted his famous caramel corn. Right next door, much like the setup at the Lazy Bee, sat a Union 76 gas station.

When David first began helping out Uncle Earl, he made a unique modification to his car: he took the backseat out and stored it in his garage, creating space to transport even more popcorn for deliveries. At the time, David was attending UCLA, balancing his studies and this popcorn business. One particular day, he remembers parking on the third floor of the campus garage with 402 bags of "Big Dave's Popped Popcorn" loaded in his car. Exhausted, he decided to take a quick nap before his next class. Rolling down the passenger window for a bit of air, he leaned back, and just ten minutes later, out of the corner of his eye, he spotted a fellow student sneaking up to grab a bag. David yelled, "Hey, what are you doing?" That marked the last time he left his windows down during a nap.

David's days were grueling, starting at 5:30 a.m. and ending after midnight. He'd deliver to liquor stores, some of which stayed open until 2 a.m. The long hours left little time for rest, but the business needed every bit of dedication he could muster.

One memorable day, while on campus headed to the student bookstore, David saw a towering figure—7'2", to be exact—coming his way. He would later regret not saying hello to Kareem Abdul-Jabbar, who was known as Ferdinand Lewis Alcindor Jr. back then, or simply, Lew Alcindor. Walking into the bookstore, David often noticed a woman with dark hair who gave everyone the "fish eye." He had his suspicions about her honesty, and, in a strange twist, he later read in the LA Times that she'd been arrested for embezzlement.

David also recalls Jack Hirsch, a UCLA Bruin, who married David's next-door neighbor, Lynn. Jack's family had gone into the pornography business, and Jack once commented that it was "infinitely cleaner" than college recruiting. Jack himself went on to make millions in the family's bowling business.

Uncle Earl's plan for David was to focus on sales and deliveries. Their flagship product was a high-class gourmet nut corn, brimming with almonds, cashews, and pecans. They sold it to upscale drug stores with candy sections, to gift shops, and to prominent liquor stores like Mac's Liquors on Wilshire Boulevard in Beverly Hills. Mac's and its sister stores, including Century Liquor, expanded every two years as the three partners would invest in a new location.

David's largest client was an upscale supermarket that sold their nut corn in the bakery section, not on the regular snack shelves, a placement that highlighted the product's exclusive appeal. Then one day, David received a call from the bakery buyer: the latest order was infested with bugs. Not only would they not pay for it, but David had to pick it up. This setback hit hard, but even more trouble loomed.

A typhoon in the Philippines caused coconut oil, a crucial ingredient to make popcorn, to skyrocket in price. Overnight, the cost quadrupled. The combined blows from the bug incident and the oil crisis eventually pushed Big Dave's Popcorn off the map, marking the end of an era in David's journey.

The Start of an Empire

David followed his Uncle Earl into the dynamic and ambitious world of Central Purchasing, a company that would later be known as Harbor Freight. Located on Wyandotte Street in North Hollywood, California, it was a humble setup, but the place thrived with energy. David's uncle, the manager, had hired him as one of the first employees, putting him at the heart of the company's foundational years. His job? Work the yellow pages.

Central Purchasing had an extensive collection of yellow page directories, sourced from cities and states across the entire country. Alongside these, they used Dun & Bradstreet index cards, which listed phone numbers, addresses, and classifications of businesses. They targeted specific industries—electrical contractors, plumbing contractors, home builders, and essentially anyone who might use extension cords. These cords, along with masking tape, electrostatic copy paper, and a knockoff version of Xerox toner, became the backbone of Central Purchasing's initial product line.

The office setup was modest yet purposeful, with eight men working in their individual cubicles in the front building. A warehouse in the back held their inventory, while each salesman manned a Wat's Line phone—a line that allowed for unlimited long-distance calls at a flat rate, the precursor to modern toll-free numbers. Each salesman had an alias: David took on the name "Dave Collins," and his coworkers included a "Paul Fern," "George Allen" (named after the then-current coach of the Rams), and "Earl Byrd" for his uncle, a playful twist on "the early bird gets the worm." Earl opened the office each morning at 4:30 a.m., ready for the East Coast market when it was 7:30 a.m. in New York, as contractors were known to start early.

Armed with scripts, each salesman knew their pitch by heart. A classic line involved a supposed government cancellation at Lockheed Aircraft, where, they claimed, 105 fifty-foot, three-prong extension cords had to be liquidated at an unbeatable price. But David, who wasn't especially handy, felt out of place discussing tools. Instead, he specialized in electrostatic copy paper, a coated paper that felt slightly damp to the touch. Since Xerox dominated the market, this copy paper was both unique and affordable, and it became a highly successful item for Central Purchasing.

As David walked by each cubicle, he couldn't help but overhear the audacious sales tactics of his colleagues. They spun stories that went beyond standard pitches. One salesman, for instance, told a customer he'd lost his legs in Vietnam, implying that a phone job was all he could get. Another bragged about selling a customer 10,000 sheets of electrostatic copy paper, only to call back days later to offer "just one last batch" of an additional 10,000 sheets. The salesmen had even been instructed to imply that they were from Xerox itself, opening calls by casually asking, "How's your Xerox toner supply?" to subtly make customers believe they were talking to Xerox representatives.

One day, David entered the office of "Smitty," the company's owner. Smitty was well-liked, a genuine and kind man who inspired loyalty from his employees. It wasn't surprising that Smitty would later pass the company to his son, who would eventually grow Harbor Freight into a nationwide powerhouse.

David approached Smitty with an idea. "About two blocks from here is a company called Ideal," he suggested. "They sell paint roller covers. I think we could do well with those." Intrigued, Smitty visited Ideal two days later and secured a distributorship. The paint covers became a massive success, adding an entirely new product line to Central Purchasing's catalog.

Another day, David had an epiphany and found himself once again in Smitty's office. "Smitty," he said, leaning in with a grin, "I think I know your secret. I figured out how you choose which cities to call each day."

Smitty's eyebrows shot up in surprise. "No way," he replied, leaning back, a mix of amusement and skepticism on his face. "Nobody knows that. Not even my wife."

But David continued, explaining that he'd been checking the national weather section in the LA Times every morning, zeroing in on cities with warm but moderate weather and clear skies. These were cities where people were likely to be in a good mood, receptive to a sales pitch. Smitty looked at him, half in amazement and half in disbelief.

"How did you know that?" he finally said, laughing. "Don't tell anyone—that's been my best sales secret for years."

With a wink, David agreed to keep it under wraps. But now, fifty years later, the secret could finally be shared. That little office on Wyandotte Street had grown into a retail empire, with over 1,500 stores across 48 states and a valuation surpassing $8 billion. The journey began in a modest room, armed with yellow pages, audacious pitches, and the intuition of a few salesmen ready to take on the world.

Break a Leg

David's Uncle Earl came to him one day with an interesting proposition. Earl's best friend, Hal, who had known David for years, wanted to talk to him about a new business venture. When David met with Hal, he was told of a plan that seemed almost too good to be true. Hal proposed a partnership where he would supply the building, capital for inventory, order processing, and customer credit. All David had to do was help sell electrostatic paper to any business with a copy machine, and they would split the profits 50-50. David was intrigued, though something about it felt off—deals that seem too good to be true usually are. But he agreed to give it a try.

On the first night of the new business, David and Hal made a late-night visit to one of their competitors. At 3 a.m., they found themselves dumpster diving in a public alley, gathering old envelopes and used pink "while you were gone" memo notes. Most of the envelopes contained return addresses, a goldmine for leads. Back at the office, they sorted through their findings, now armed with enough contacts to get started. They quickly built up a customer base, though David had the sense that their methods might not exactly be legal today.

David hit the ground running, landing orders from notable clients. TRW purchased 200 rolls of copy paper, while Revel, the toy company, ordered 100 rolls. Sam's U-Drive not only bought 100 rolls but also purchased a used copier from David. He remembered hauling it up a flight of stairs with Hal muttering, "It's not worth this kind of money to do this much work." Every week, sales increased. Ironically, the only sale Hal made was to his insurance company, and they soon returned the product, claiming it had damaged their machine.

One Friday, David walked into the office a bit after 10 a.m., noting the clock. Hal was waiting, and David could tell something was wrong. With a stone-faced expression, Hal said only two words, "That's it." Handing over a check for $850, Hal announced he was closing this part of the business. Hal said it was taking too much time away from his alloy business. David took the check and left.

Afterward, David called Doug Danes, a broker for West Virginia Pulp and Paper, which supplied their copy paper. He explained Hal's departure from the business and asked if he could continue buying paper at the same rate, $5.50 per roll. Doug agreed, and David took the opportunity to launch his own business, Collins Office Supplies.

As Collins took off, David expanded his product line. He became a distributor for Avery Labels, receiving generous discounts. Soon, he was also distributing Bic pens, with their popular four-color, spring-loaded ballpoint pen—a hit among nurses for easy color-coding. David loved the product, especially its French craftsmanship. He also became a distributor for the Fisher Pen Company, known for their "astronaut pen" that could write upside down and in space. Finally, he added Ready Form Office Supplies to his list, and within a few months, Collins Office Supplies was thriving.

But David's success hadn't gone unnoticed. One day, he received a call from Herb, Hal's partner in his alloy business. Herb claimed David was now competing directly with them, despite Hal's earlier statement that they were leaving the copy paper industry. Herb, in a sharp tone, threatened, "If you continue in this business, I'll send two guys over to break your legs."

Calmly, David hung up. An hour later, he called Herb back, informing him that he had reported the threat to the Van Nuys Police Department. He wanted Herb to know that if anything happened to him, the police would know where to look.

With that chapter closed, David continued running Collins Office Supplies successfully for another six months before heading off to basic training at Fort Polk, Louisiana.

I'm in the Army Now

David remembers the day he signed up for the Army with a mix of clarity and disbelief. He went to the draft board on Colfax Avenue in North Hollywood, California, determined to find a role that suited his skills and interests. He specifically requested an MOS (Military Occupational Specialty) related to bookkeeping or business. But, in a twist that would shape his service, he was assigned as a medic instead—a job he would never have chosen, especially given his traumatic past.

As a five-year-old, David had been involved in a household accident that left lasting scars. One day, full of energy and innocence, he ran straight into a closed glass patio door, thinking it was open. The impact left him bleeding and frightened. Fortunately, a quick-thinking neighbor, Mr. Milstein, heard his mother's screams and rushed over, quickly driving them to the emergency room, where David needed 36 stitches. His mother's spotless housekeeping had made that glass door look invisible, a household hazard that left him with not only physical scars but also a deep-seated fear of medical situations. That old wound would occasionally remind him of itself, as a small piece of glass lodged in his left hand would resurface now and then—a memento of his first encounter with trauma.

After receiving his orders, David found himself on a plane to Fort Polk, Louisiana, a training camp known for preparing men for Vietnam. During his flight, he tripped on an escalator and tore his jeans around the knee. Looking down at his ripped jeans, he couldn't help but think, "Is this the start of a bad dream?"

As soon as David stepped off the bus at Fort Polk, a drill sergeant with a thick Southern accent zeroed in on him, barking, "Fat boy, we're going to take some weight off of you!" The sergeant informed him he'd be allowed only two meals a day and assigned him as the road guard, meaning he'd have to run ahead of the troop during marches to signal oncoming traffic. The rigors of training were tough on David, who had always been somewhat uncoordinated. He'd struggled with basic motor skills as a kid and didn't learn to tie his shoes until he was seven, so he knew he had his work cut out for him.

David's time at Fort Polk brought not only physical challenges but also moments of connection with his fellow soldiers. Every morning at roll call, he'd notice his buddy Steve, who'd been receiving regular mail from his wife during the first three weeks of training. Then, suddenly, Steve stopped getting letters. Concerned, David mentioned it to him, and Steve shared that he was going through marital problems. David was the only one who had noticed and cared enough to ask. Steve confided in David, grateful that someone had paid enough attention to realize something was wrong.

The weeks at Fort Polk became a blur of physical tests and challenges. The base was hit by an outbreak of spinal meningitis, which only heightened the tense atmosphere. Then came the dreaded gas chamber drill, where trainees were instructed to enter a room, remove their gas masks, and endure the effects of tear gas. Luckily, David was scheduled for kitchen duty that day and spent his time peeling potatoes. Relieved, he thought he'd managed to escape the exercise. But two weeks later, he was called back in to complete it, making him wish he'd never known what he was missing.

One memorable event came on payday. Most of the young men in David's unit were fresh out of high school, still unused to getting a regular paycheck. David, a bit older than the rest after six years at UCLA, watched with amusement as some of his fellow soldiers received their pay in green cash. For a few of them, it seemed like the first time they'd held real money in their hands, and they reacted as though it were a rare treasure. Some even lifted the bills to their noses, breathing in the scent as if savoring something entirely new. To David, it was a funny reminder of how different he was from the others—he'd seen his share of cash before, but watching these young men revel in the feeling of a real paycheck was an unexpected source of camaraderie.

Then, during a physical assessment, David was faced with events that tested his coordination. He managed to run a mile in eight minutes and thirty seconds, navigate the monkey bars, and attempt the low crawl—an obstacle he simply couldn't conquer. Determined to help, his friend Peter switched shirts with him and completed the low crawl in David's place, allowing David to pass the test. If he had failed, he would have had to start training all over again. David had given up his office supply business to join the Army and was desperate to finish basic training and get back to it as quickly as possible.

The Army experience sparked an idea David couldn't shake: a restaurant concept he'd call "The Mess Hall." He imagined it as a fun, Army-style dining experience with staff dressed like drill sergeants who'd make sarcastic comments like, "Do you really need all that food?" Diners would sign in just as they would in the Army, eat iconic military dishes like "Shit on a Shingle" (creamed beef on toast), and might even have to drop and give ten push-ups if they got too rowdy. To-go containers would be called "MREs," and once in a while, customers would be asked to march through the restaurant chanting a cadence. David believed it would be a huge hit, as long as the food was good and the military nostalgia was in full effect.

In the midst of basic training, David learned about an earthquake that had struck the San Fernando Valley, where his family lived. He tried calling home repeatedly from a payphone but couldn't reach anyone, and as he heard rumors that the quake had been centered near his neighborhood, his worry grew. The next day, a sympathetic officer allowed him to use the office phone. David finally got through, relieved to hear his mother's voice on the line. She told him that they were all okay, though the house was in shambles.

After graduating from basic training, David was sent to Fort Sam Houston in San Antonio, Texas, for his medical training. There, he had a few days off to visit the Alamo and stroll the River Walk, where a local pimp approached him. Until that moment, David had never seriously considered hiring a prostitute, but curiosity got the better of him, and he struck up a conversation.

"How much?" David asked, unsure of the going rate.

The man replied, "Twenty bucks."

David looked around nervously. "And how long do I have?"

The man smirked, "Till you've finished."

David thought about it, but in the end, he decided it wasn't worth the risk of being caught by the military police and quickly walked away. That conversation stayed with him as a strange memory of Fort Sam.

One day, he took a Greyhound bus home for Christmas, only to sit too close to the bus's exhaust fumes, which made for the most nauseating ride of his life. Another vivid memory from Fort Sam was an unusual medical exercise where he and his buddy had to take each other's temperatures using rectal thermometers—an experience that, for David, was as awkward as it was memorable.

Later in his Army career, while at summer camp in TwentyNine Palms, California, David received an urgent call from his wife, Rebecca, saying that her water had broken. With no one around to grant him leave, David made a snap decision and left the camp on his own to be by her side. He arrived at the hospital just in time to witness the birth of his son, Bert. A couple of days later, the Red Cross informed him he'd been marked as AWOL (Absent Without Leave). When he explained the situation to Army headquarters, they showed understanding and let him make up the time.

On the day he shipped out from Fort Polk to begin advanced medical training at Fort Sam, David took a moment to shake his drill sergeant's hand. He looked him in the eye and said, "Thank you, Drill Sergeant. I've lost 45 pounds because of your efforts. I've never been in this great of shape in my life." David thinks it was the only time anyone ever thanked that sergeant for the rigorous training.

Looking back on it all, David has come to appreciate those challenging days. He faced fears, physical tests, and all kinds of encounters, from childhood accidents to drill sergeants, friendships to earthquake scares. And who knows? Maybe one day, that "Mess Hall" restaurant will become a reality, complete with military nostalgia, good food, and a touch of marching-cadence fun for all.

Help spread the word about this book!

If you enjoyed it, please consider sharing it on social media or recommending it on platforms where books are discovered and sold. If you are an influencer, or know someone who is, we'd be thrilled if you shared it with your audience. Every mention helps new readers discover the story and supports David Klein's mission to pay off The Jelly Belly Candy Company. Thank you for being a part of this journey!

Rebecca, Oh Rebecca

Rebecca Klein

David Klein first met Rebecca under somewhat unusual circumstances. While stationed as a medic at Los Angeles General Hospital with the Army, he often wandered out during his lunch break, always at exactly 12:05 PM, looking for something to eat. One fateful day, he ventured across the street to a small store. There, he encountered a man who left a lasting impression—a tall, mustached figure named Ben who had an eccentric air about him but exuded a certain kindness. Ben's shop was unique in its own right, sourcing candy primarily from Jack's Candy in Los Angeles, which specialized in close-out items. The place had a quirky charm.

As David browsed through the aisles, Ben observed him in his white medic attire. Assuming David was a doctor, Ben struck up a conversation, likely with an eye to introducing his daughter to a potential match. After a few exchanges, Ben casually mentioned that his daughter, Rebecca, was studying in England to become a teacher. He must have seen some spark in David, as he handed over a scrap of paper with Rebecca's phone number on it, advising David to call her once she was back in town, about two months from then.

True to his word, two months later, David gave Rebecca a call the day she returned from England. Their first date was unforgettable: they went to the Troubadour, a legendary Los Angeles venue, to watch performances by Helen Reddy and the Nitty Gritty Dirt Band. This magical evening marked the beginning of a lifelong connection that would only grow stronger with time. Within a year, David and Rebecca were married.

Rebecca wasn't just a supportive partner; she quickly became an invaluable ally in David's business ventures. During the early days of the Jelly Belly business, an order of 30 pounds each of eight flavors arrived from Goelitz Confectionery Company (later renamed Jelly Belly Candy Company). However, the beans had a critical flaw: five of the flavors were so stuck together that pulling them apart risked damaging the beans and leaving unsightly pockmarks. Rebecca had a bright idea to salvage the batch. She suggested spreading the beans on cake sheets and setting them in the sun. As they warmed, the beans softened, making them easy to separate without damage. Her quick thinking saved what would become one of the most iconic candy brands in America.

Before Jelly Belly, however, Rebecca had already been contributing to the Klein family's business efforts. At the time, David and Rebecca were running a wholesale nut business, supplying primarily to bakeries in the San Gabriel Valley. David would make his rounds, lugging 25-pound boxes of light walnut halves and pieces, while Rebecca stayed behind in the car, guarding their cargo. In the heat of California summers, temperatures could easily soar above 100 degrees. With the windows open because the air conditioning was not working, Rebecca kept the nuts safe from overheating—a critical factor, as raw walnuts could quickly become infested with larvae in high temperatures. David often shared this story as a piece of advice for future food entrepreneurs, urging them to roast or freeze their walnuts to prevent infestations.

After they were married, David and Rebecca didn't have the chance to go on a traditional honeymoon. David had to return to law school on Monday, so they spent the day after their wedding strolling down Colorado Boulevard in Pasadena. They caught a showing of *Snoopy, Come Home*, a Peanuts movie. Afterward, they visited a health food store called House of Nutrition, one of California's first. The owner, a kindly woman, was immediately taken with Rebecca. She later confided in David, telling him that Rebecca had a unique quality about her—an aura of innocence that made a lasting impression.

David and Rebecca dreamed of a family with two children—a boy and a girl—and that dream came true. Their first home was a small apartment on Ardmore Avenue in Los Angeles, near David's law school. The rent was a manageable $200 a month, and David remembers studying for exams in the bathtub, where he found a quiet refuge from distractions. He would immerse himself in the warmth and dive into Gilbert's books on contracts. On one memorable Saturday afternoon, as he was deeply engrossed in his studies, there was a knock at the door. It was the apartment manager, complaining about water leaking into the unit below. Although David doesn't remember how he resolved the situation, he recalls the peculiar feeling of studying in that cozy tub.

Years later, during a family stay at a hotel near Magic Mountain, David found himself in a similar predicament, falling asleep in the bathroom and accidentally flooding the floor. He spent the better part of the evening using every towel in the room to soak up the water. Despite the occasional mishap, these memories became cherished moments, etched in his mind.

David's walks to law school, about two and a half miles each way, also became a source of inspiration. He would pass by various small stores, delighting in their unique displays. One store, in particular, stood out: an Allen Wertz candy shop known for its handmade chocolates. On his way home one day, he stopped in and bought a small bag of miniature jelly beans, unaware of how this seemingly insignificant purchase would foreshadow his future. Allen Wertz would eventually become a distributor of David's Jelly Belly jelly beans, although their buyer, Deloris, initially resisted the price for the licorice-flavored beans. Her knowledge of Herman Goelitz's previous mini jelly beans allowed her to negotiate a lower price, taking advantage of the situation that David respected as a shrewd business move.

Rebecca's unwavering support for their family business continued throughout their marriage. David later realized that Rebecca had never signed away her share of the Jelly Belly ownership when they sold it, a detail that became significant in hindsight. For years, Rebecca expressed dissatisfaction with the sale, often insisting that she still had a rightful claim to the brand. When she passed away in 2020, David was reminded of California's community property laws, which entitled her to an equal share of all assets acquired during their marriage. His business partner Cal's wife had signed off on her share, but, curiously, Rebecca never did.

Rebecca's passing during the height of the COVID-19 pandemic was especially difficult. She spent her final months in a rehab facility, and due to strict protocols, David wasn't allowed to visit in person. Instead, he called daily, often waiting hours just for a few brief moments with her. These calls became a lifeline, a precious connection during an incredibly isolating time. David still misses Rebecca deeply, particularly the way she showered love on their children, the family they had built together.

Rebecca's presence was—and still is—felt in every aspect of David's life and career. Her intuition and ingenuity not only saved their early business ventures but shaped the course of their lives. David's admiration for her is undiminished, his memories of her vibrant and alive.

The Light bulb Moment

David was relaxing alone in his living room one evening. His wife, Rebecca, with their son, Bert, had gone to a La Leche League meeting. The house was quiet, and David found himself deep in thought. It had been a while since he felt a true creative spark, and tonight his mind wandered, considering possibilities beyond his current ventures. Then, like a flash of inspiration, an idea formed. *What if candy could be more than just a sugar fix? What if it could be an experience, something natural, something unforgettable?*

A memory flooded back from a couple years prior, when David had strolled through Allen Wertz Candy Store in Los Angeles. Amidst the colorful sea of confections, he'd spotted an unusual little jelly bean. It was a spark of intrigue then, but tonight, the idea matured into something more defined. He thought, *What if these jelly beans could be made as natural as possible? What if each one had pure fruit flavors, beautiful natural colors, and a burst of taste that went beyond anything out there?* This was it—the light bulb moment. He could practically taste the possibilities.

David's vision grew rapidly, as if it had been waiting, building up steam for this exact moment. He imagined a tiny jelly bean packed with real fruit purees in vibrant, unique flavors, each one a little treasure of sweetness. One flavor popped into his mind right away: watermelon. It would be special, a bean that not only tasted like watermelon on the inside but also had a pink center and a green shell to complete the look and flavor. Most jelly beans were just sugary fillings with a bit of flavor on the outside; but David's would be a revolution, capturing the essence of real fruit in every bite.

That evening at 6:30, David called Herm Rowland at Herman Goelitz, an established confectionery known for their mini jelly beans. David explained his idea to Herm, detailing every aspect, from the natural fruit purees to the colors that would match the flavors. He could practically feel Herm's curiosity piquing over the line. *Could Herman Goelitz make these?* David asked. *Would they create this new kind of jelly bean?*

After a pause, Herm said he'd take the order and would get to work on David's creation. Within three weeks, David's dream jelly beans arrived, neatly packed and full of promise. He opened one of the boxes, popping a watermelon jelly bean into his mouth. It was exactly as he had imagined—bursting with real flavor and a vibrant personality all its own. David would direct Herm to put less acid and to dry them longer in his Jelly Belly Jelly Beans so that they wouldn't stick together in future orders.

With his product in hand, David knew he needed the right venue, a place that was bustling, open year-round, and perhaps even frequented by celebrities. He immediately thought of Fosselman's Ice Cream in Alhambra, a popular spot with just the kind of exposure he needed. Fosselman's was a current customer of David's. David was supplying them with their nuts for their ice cream. When he walked into Fosselman's, he spotted the perfect little corner for his display and approached Bob and Jim, the owners. Bob had been using the corner to display all his awards for their outstanding ice cream. They struck a deal: Fosselman's would receive 50% of the sales from each Jelly Belly sold in exchange for rent and utilities. David knew it was steep, but it was worth the exposure.

With his corner established, David prepared for his first day at Fosselman's. That Saturday morning, he arrived at 7 a.m. to set up, carefully placing each jelly bean and getting everything just right. His parents, ever supportive, wanted him to be successful—even though they'd initially dreamed he'd be an attorney. David had studied law and even took the bar exam, but halfway through the test, he knew his heart wasn't in it. The candy business was his true calling, and nothing was going to keep him from it. Yet, he couldn't shake the feeling of doubt as he overheard his parents question his decision: "What is he doing with these beans?" It stung, but David pushed forward, determined to make them proud.

The first customer that morning was a familiar face—Rebecca's ceramic teacher. She ordered four pounds of Jelly Bellies, and as David carefully weighed the beans on his Toledo scale, a scoopful slipped and scattered across the floor. He laughed it off, muttering, "I guess I'm literally spilling the beans." Embarrassing, maybe, but it was also a lesson in humility and the little hiccups that come with any new venture. David swept up the mess, tossed the spilled beans, and refocused on his goal.

In those early days, sales were slow, sometimes only reaching $10 a day. David knew he needed a breakthrough and decided to call the Associated Press office in Los Angeles, asking to speak with the business editor. They initially suggested the food editor, but David insisted, explaining that he wanted to reach business owners who might put

Jelly Bellies in their stores. Eventually, they connected him with Steve Fox, a young journalist who was intrigued by David's pitch.

When Steve arrived that Sunday morning, he was met with a line of people stretching out the door. He seemed taken aback. "Are they always here this early?" he asked, amazed by the scene. David chuckled and replied, "You should see it in a couple of hours." What Steve didn't know was that most of the people in line were friends and family David had asked to show up to help create a buzz.

The gamble worked. Within days, the *LA Times*, *Chicago Tribune*, and other major newspapers had picked up Steve's article, spreading the word about the Jelly Belly craze sweeping Alhambra. Calls began flooding into Fosselman's, and one day, David picked up the phone to find the head candy buyer from Marshall Field's in Chicago on the line. The buyer was ready to place a massive order—$20,000 worth, a fortune in those days. However, there was one snag: David didn't have the cash flow to pay Herman Goelitz within 20 days for such a large quantity.

But the buyer came through with a solution, promising to expedite payment as soon as the product reached Chicago. Unfortunately, when the shipment arrived, there was an oversight. Herman Goelitz had drop-shipped the order directly to Chicago, but they failed to follow the buyer's instruction to put the purchase order number on each box. As per the agreement, this resulted in an automatic fine of $1,500 deducted from David's payment. David was disappointed, but he learned from the experience, vowing to keep an eye on every detail going forward.

Back at Fosselman's, David continued selling his jelly beans one by one. One afternoon, a young boy rode up on his bicycle and sampled a strawberry-flavored Jelly Belly. David asked what he thought of it, and the boy grinned, replying, "It tastes like cotton candy!" Inspired, David immediately changed the flavor name on the board to "Cotton Candy," crediting his young customer for the perfect description.

As the Jelly Belly business gained momentum, David realized that his light bulb moment had become much more than just a simple inspiration. It was a passion, a purpose, and the beginning of a journey that was just getting started.

Be Careful Out There

In the world of candy, David Klein grew up with a sense of camaraderie and mutual support. If you had asked him about the candy industry in its early days, he'd have told you it was a close-knit business, where each factory owner looked out for the interests of others. For instance, it was commonplace for other candy makers to step in and offer their facilities if a factory burned down, helping the affected owner stay afloat. "These days are definitely over with," David would say later with regret. As he learned first-hand, the candy industry had shifted, becoming a competitive landscape where ideas and opportunities could be lost or stolen in a heartbeat. Each experience taught him hard but invaluable lessons, shaping not only his career but his outlook on trust and resilience.

One of the most painful lessons David learned came during a venture he had high hopes for. He'd developed a new kind of candy gum—innovative, with ingredients and processes he carefully designed. He submitted his idea and ingredients to a potential contract manufacturer, confident in their partnership. But instead of creating the product for him, they took his concept, produced the candy themselves, and released it under their own brand. The candy went on to become a sensation, selling millions of dollars and eventually being acquired by a major company—a name nearly everyone knows. David never saw a single penny from the success of his stolen idea. The experience shattered his trust, showing him that while he might believe in the old values of mutual respect, others saw his ideas as something to exploit. The lesson was harsh: in this new era, even the most innovative ideas weren't safe without protection when just sharing your concept. He hopes other new inventors will learn from his experiences.

Another moment that tested David's moral compass and optimism came early in the Jelly Belly journey. He had struck a contract with Herm Rowland, the owner of Herman Goelitz, to produce Jelly Belly jelly beans, and initially, the arrangement was smooth. Goelitz charged him 59 cents per pound plus shipping from Oakland, California, to his base in South El Monte. When demand for Jelly Bellies began to skyrocket, David didn't wait for Herm to request an increase. Instead, he picked up the phone and offered a voluntary price hike, proposing a 10-cent increase per pound. Herm was taken aback and asked if David wanted the change to apply to the 40,000-pound shipment due the next day. Without hesitation, David confirmed. It was an additional $4,000 on that bill alone—a considerable sum in the early days of Jelly Belly. David's decision was unheard of, an example of loyalty in a business that had already begun to favor profit over principles. But it taught him, too, that such gestures were increasingly rare and often went unreciprocated.

To secure his place in the industry, David later attempted to create his own candy factory, hoping to control the production and direction of his products. When a man, impressed by David's story and his dreams, reached out offering partnership and support, David welcomed him. Together, they discussed ideas, and David poured his heart into developing new products. Among them was *Spanks*, a candy David had featured in his documentary, which quickly gained traction. The man expressed interest in distributing it, so David shared his processes and marketing insights openly, hoping they could grow the brand together.

But soon, David's excitement turned into another devastating blow. Without warning, the man filed a federal trademark for *Spanks* under his own name and sent David a cease-and-desist letter, barring him from selling his own creation. What had started as an inspiring partnership left David once again grappling with betrayal. He'd shared his ideas in good faith, only to see them weaponized against him. It was a reminder that even when intentions seemed genuine, one wrong step could cost him dearly.

Despite the setback, David still clung to his hope of creating a new product with his name on it. This same man approached David with another proposal: a signature jelly bean bearing David's name and a fair percentage of the profits going his way. With cautious optimism, David agreed. They placed an order with a third-party manufacturer David had worked with for years, and David arranged for Garvey Nut—a prominent distributor he once owned and later sold to Steve Corri—to become the master U.S. distributor for the beans. Garvey's distribution strength could have guaranteed a successful launch.

But the venture met an insurmountable challenge. Shortly before the jelly beans were set to launch, Garvey's representatives were confronted by an employee from Jelly Belly Candy Company at a trade show. The message was stark: if Garvey distributed these signature jelly beans, they would lose the right to sell Jelly Belly products. Jelly Belly was synonymous with quality and reliability in the candy industry, and for Garvey, losing that brand was too great a risk. Steve Corri, understanding the implications, informed David they'd have to step back from the venture, leaving David with a warehouse full of unsold beans and a shattered plan.

Determined to seek justice, David reported the incident to the Department of Justice's Antitrust Division. Investigators interviewed everyone involved, but after a lengthy wait, David's Freedom of Information Act request returned a heavily redacted document, its pages filled with blacked-out lines, offering no insights or closure. Garvey sat on the merchandise for years without paying for the merchandise, eventually selling it to a close-out company, and David was left to wonder how things might have been different in an ethical world.

Each painful lesson left an indelible mark, but David adapted by learning to lean on his own resilience, ingenuity, and an inner belief that he could keep moving forward, even when trust was shattered. The old way of the candy industry he loved was gone—replaced by a landscape where ideas were currency and everyone guarded their secrets. David's experiences taught him more than just business acumen; they taught him the importance of protecting his ideas and never relying too fully on another's goodwill. In a world that had turned cutthroat, David Klein continued to adapt, growing tougher and wiser with each experience, determined to keep making his mark, even when faced with betrayal.

A Sweet Beginning on Ventura Boulevard

In the summer of 1977, the sweltering heat of the San Fernando Valley baked the streets of Sherman Oaks. David, a young entrepreneur with a knack for innovation and a love for all things sweet, was heading home from his parents' house. His car cruised along Ventura Boulevard, the artery connecting Studio City and Sherman Oaks. It was a bustling thoroughfare teeming with life—a mix of locals, tourists, and the occasional celebrity weaving through the vibrant neighborhood.

David's mind buzzed with thoughts about his store, The Jelly Belly. Nestled in the heart of a growing candy market, the store had quickly become a local favorite. As he passed block after block of storefronts and eateries, a bright "For Lease" sign caught his eye. The address, 12350 Ventura Boulevard, was easy to remember. It was located next to The Scoreboard, a popular sports apparel shop, and just a short stroll from his go-to spot, Art's Deli.

Art's Deli was more than just a place to grab a bite—it was a landmark. Known for their slogan, "Every sandwich is a work of Art," they proudly displayed mouthwatering images of towering sandwiches on their walls. The deli was a hub for celebrities, thanks to its proximity to CBS Studios. David had spent countless afternoons there, marveling at the sandwich artistry, indulging in oversized portions, and people-watching as stars filtered in and out.

The location felt serendipitous. Ventura Boulevard was alive with opportunity, and the address had a rhythm to it, one that resonated with David's aspirations. Without hesitation, he jotted down the number on the "For Lease" sign and began imagining the possibilities.

Several months later, The Jelly Belly opened to rave reviews. The store's layout became a candy-lover's dream. David, ever the visionary, installed massive lucite tubes along one wall, filling them with every flavor of Jelly Belly jelly beans imaginable. The display was both practical and eye-catching, inviting customers to scoop their favorites into bags with a delightful sense of autonomy. It was a concept ahead of its time, setting the standard for candy stores everywhere.

David didn't stop at jelly beans. He sought out the finest candies from around the world. Among them was his personal favorite: Swedish Fish. Back then, the chewy treats were still imported from Sweden, made by the Malaco Company and distributed in the U.S. by the Jaret Candy Company. The red Swedish Fish, with its subtle lingonberry flavor, held a special place in David's heart. To him, they were superior in taste and texture compared to modern iterations.

Every week, David and his family would gather in the back of the store, wash their hands, and perform an unusual yet effective ritual—they'd separate the assorted Swedish Fish into single-color piles by hand. Customers were thrilled to see the vibrantly separated candies, an offering they couldn't find anywhere else. David often indulged in his favorite combination: one orange and one red Swedish Fish eaten together, a pairing that evoked the nostalgic taste of a summer popsicle.

The Jelly Belly quickly became more than just a candy store; it was a cultural hub. Families wandered in on weekends, children's eyes widening at the sight of over 400 varieties of candy from across the globe. It was a place where nostalgia mingled with novelty, and the self-service model gave customers a sense of playful freedom.

Celebrities were among its regular patrons. The great Frank Sinatra himself loved to stock up on chocolate licorice, a delicacy he adored. He loved it so much that he had it shipped regularly to his home in Palm Springs.

Parking at the store was its only drawback. With limited spots in the back and high demand for street parking, some customers found it challenging. But David's ingenuity knew no bounds. He turned every potential setback into an opportunity, encouraging mail-order business for loyal customers who couldn't make it to the store.

Word spread quickly. Ventura Boulevard, already a vibrant hub, now boasted a candy store unlike any other. David's passion for quality and his innovative approach to customer experience set The Jelly Belly apart. The store wasn't just a place to buy candy—it was an experience, a trip down memory lane for adults and a whimsical adventure for kids.

Years later, people would reminisce about The Jelly Belly with warmth and affection. The lucite tube displays, the separated Swedish Fish, and the countless candies lining the walls became iconic in the community. David had created something timeless, a legacy built on sweetness and innovation.

And it all started on Ventura Boulevard, with a single sign and a vision.

Sticky Fingers

The year was 1977, a time of transformation for a little retail store located at 9533 E. Garvey in South El Monte, California. The store was a modest space but brimming with charm and entrepreneurial spirit. It was here that David first met Cal, a meeting that would shape the store's destiny. Cal's parents owned the property, and their familial investment in the place gave it an air of stability. Yet, it was David's ingenuity that began to carve out its niche in the bustling community.

At first glance, the store seemed like any other small-town shop. Shelves lined with neatly packaged nuts in every variety imaginable. Customers wandered through its aisles, enticed by the rich, roasted aroma of pecans, almonds, and macadamias. But behind the scenes, the operation was already adapting to challenges. The health department had once informed them that storing extra boxes of nuts within the store itself was a violation. Unfazed, they built a space behind the retail store to comply, complete with a walk-in box where chocolates could be kept cool. Without it, the relentless California heat would have melted the delicate treats, leaving them covered in an unsightly white haze known as "bloom." Though harmless, it was a blemish that customers avoided.

David soon saw the potential for growth. The walk-in box was just the beginning. As business expanded, Cal added another building to accommodate their growing inventory. While the store was open seven days a week, David spent most of his time delivering nuts to customers, including notable names like Famous Amos. Still, his occasional presence in the store left an impression.

One such day, around 1 p.m., David was at the counter when he noticed a man in a brown sports jacket slipping a half-pound package of roasted and salted macadamia nuts into his pocket. Macadamia nuts were a luxury item, meticulously packaged in half-pound bags due to their expense. Calm but firm, David approached the man and casually mentioned that he had to leave for court in an hour to prosecute a shoplifter. The thief froze, his face a picture of surprise and guilt. Though he didn't return the nuts, he never returned to the store either—a small victory in retail justice.

The store wasn't just a business; it was a community hub, a place of innovation and warmth. Customers marveled at the fresh peanut butter machine, a marvel crafted by the Grindmaster company. Customers could drop in a quarter, and the machine would churn out creamy peanut butter while playing a whimsical tune: "Peanut, Peanut Butter," a song by The Marathons. This touch of novelty brought smiles to the faces of visitors and was a testament to David's knack for creating memorable experiences. The peanuts for this machine came from a supplier in downtown Los Angeles, a man named Morris Rosenberg who specialized in a unique grade of peanuts.

Beyond the gadgets, the store's organization reflected a deep understanding of customer preferences. Nuts were sold shelled because customers valued convenience, and the grading process ensured no fragments of shell remained—a crucial detail for home cooks and bakers. The store also had a bulk section where patrons could scoop their desired quantities, an innovation ahead of its time.

It was at this very location that David received his first shipment of Jelly Bellies, the candy that would later become a sensation. David had meticulously planned the launch of the jelly beans, aiming to make a splash in the competitive candy world. Cal, however, was frustrated when David chose Fosselman's Ice Cream in Alhambra to showcase the first sales instead of Garvey Nut House. Cal argued that the home base deserved the honor. David explained his reasoning: Alhambra was frequented by celebrities, making it a strategic choice to gain media attention and traction for the new candy.

Adding to Cal's frustration was the fact that Garvey Nut House wasn't mentioned in any of the articles covering the Jelly Belly launch. He confronted David about it, asking why the store was being overlooked. In an effort to appease Cal, David promised to take out an ad in the Los Angeles Times, stating that Jelly Bellies were available at both the Alhambra location and Garvey Nut House. The ad ran for $450, a hefty sum in those days, but David felt it was worth the investment to give Garvey its moment in the spotlight.

David vividly remembers the day when a massive shipment of Jelly Bellies arrived in 30-pound boxes. As he stood next to the towering stack, one of the bottom boxes collapsed under the weight, sending the entire pile cascading downward. In the split second that followed, David managed to move out of the way. If he hadn't, he believed he would have been crushed to death. Later, he couldn't help but think of the potential headline: "Man Crushed by His Own Invention." It was a close call, and it underscored just how unpredictable life in the candy business could be.

The holidays were especially busy at the store, with specials often featured in the local food section on Thursdays. Seasonal demand transformed the shop into a bustling hive of activity. Employees like Penny, a young mother, brought heart and dedication to the operation. One Christmas, she confided in David that she couldn't afford a tree for her child. Without hesitation, David handed her $20, a small gesture that left Penny in tears and exemplified the kindness that defined the store's culture.

Then there were Ann and Eve, two sisters who became fixtures in the Garvey Nut House family. Eve had previously worked at another store in San Marino before David's father-in-law took over. Her departure sparked an outcry from loyal customers, who frequently called David asking when Eve would return. The San Marino community's fondness for Eve contrasted sharply with their reluctance to do business with David's father-in-law, further underscoring the personal relationships that defined the store's success.

By 1979, Garvey Nut House had become a major player in the nut industry. They began doing business with Peanut Corporation of America, purchasing peanut butter stock by the truckload for distribution to ice cream shops and health food stores. David even hosted representatives from the company at the store, a meeting marked by mutual respect and optimism. Yet, decades later, the name Peanut Corporation of America would be tarnished. A devastating scandal involving contaminated products led to illness and loss of life. David, no longer involved with Garvey by then, watched in disbelief as his former business acquaintance, Stewart Parnell, faced Senate hearings and prison. The contamination resulted in the deaths of nine people and sickened over 700 others. Companies were forced to recall millions of dollars worth of products, and the tragedy left an indelible mark on the food industry.

During the Senate hearings, a chilling moment revealed Stewart's guilt and lack of accountability. A senator, holding a jar of peanut butter produced by the Peanut Corporation of America, offered Stewart a taste of his own product. Stewart refused, his hesitation speaking volumes about the product's safety. This moment became symbolic of the negligence and disregard for consumer safety that had caused so much pain and loss.

This memory was brought to the forefront of David's mind when he recently learned of another foodborne illness outbreak involving Boar's Head products. Ten people had died, and many more were sickened after consuming contaminated products. The parallels were striking and heartbreaking—a grim reminder that history could repeat itself when companies failed to prioritize safety over profit. For David, it reinforced the importance of integrity and care in the food industry, values he had always held dear.

Amid these memories, the store's legacy lived on. In later years, David returned to 9533 E. Garvey to film a segment for his documentary, Candyman: The David Klein Story. Walking through the store, he rediscovered old labels that read "Garvey Nut House," relics of a bygone era. The documentary captured the nostalgia of a time when a small business could thrive on innovation, community, and the determination of people like David.

Garvey Nut House was more than a store. It was a place where laughter mixed with the scent of roasting nuts, where ingenuity turned challenges into opportunities, and where acts of kindness left lasting impressions. Though time has passed and the world has changed, the spirit of that little store in South El Monte endures—a testament to the impact of vision, hard work, and humanity.

Cal Strikes Gold and Ben's Logic

David first met Cal during a delivery to one of his customers, Al Pearce, who ran a shop on Garvey Avenue in South El Monte. Al was a unique character who specialized in chocolate-covered prunes, attracting a local following for his sweet creations. After finishing his delivery, David noticed a small nut shop nearby, adorned with a charming logo that read "Garvey Nut House." He had extra merchandise in his car and figured, "Why not try for one more sale?" It was late in the day, but David decided to take a chance.

Inside, Cal had just returned from his day job as a high school typing teacher. He came across as a man who was comfortable enough in business but didn't seem deeply invested. David showed him the popcorn and some peanut brittle, and Cal was mildly interested. "What's my cost going to be?" he asked. David told him it was 39 cents a bag for the popcorn and made an equally appealing offer on the peanut brittle, explaining that Cal could easily double his money. Cal liked the name "Big Dave's Popcorn." Cal agreed to buy a dozen bags of each with a shrug, not seeing much risk in it.

That transaction could have been the end of it, but four years later, David returned to Garvey Nut House with a new idea: entering the wholesale nut business. Cal was surprised to see him again and asked why he hadn't returned with more popcorn. David explained about the typhoon in the Philippines and how it had destroyed the coconut oil crop, causing the market price to quadruple overnight, making popcorn production unprofitable. That setback had led him to abandon the popcorn business, but now he had a new vision.

At this time, David was finishing his final year of law school, and he laid out his proposal to Cal. "Let's start a wholesale nut business," he suggested, explaining he'd handle sales and day-to-day operations, although his legal career might eventually take precedence. Cal, who taught typing nine months out of the year, warned David he wouldn't be able to help much beyond giving access to the shop. David didn't mind; all he needed was warehouse space and Cal's line of credit to buy the nuts.

The Garvey Nut House was primarily stocked with shelled walnuts, which Cal sold to customers from his small retail store. Most of his other nut inventory came from wholesalers. But David was envisioning a larger business and saw promise in expanding their offerings. That idea was only reinforced when David's mother called one day, eager to find a wholesale source for walnuts for her baking.

David contacted the Superior Nut Company and spoke with Al Rosen, an old contact from his popcorn days. Al offered unbeatable prices on walnuts, claiming he kept over 10,000 pounds in stock at all times. Before ending the call, David asked how Al's retail store in Granada Hills was doing. Al confessed he was losing thousands each month but shrugged it off, revealing he made $20,000 monthly in the wholesale nut business.

With Cal as a passive partner, David threw himself into the wholesale nut business, handling sales and logistics. Within a few months, David had built a client base of more than fifty regular customers, selling everything from walnuts to pecans to bakeries from Solvang down to San Diego. He even secured Famous Amos and Mrs. Gooch's as clients, eventually joining the board of directors at Mrs. Gooch's. Every Friday, David's friend and co-founder of Mrs. Gooch's, Dan Volland, would drive from West L.A. to pick up his nut order, which David's mom would take by phone each Thursday.

The small general store across from L.A. General Hospital that David's father in law Ben owned, was selling a mix of artificial flowers and candy that had seen better days. Ben had his quirks, including the belief that he was helping people by offering them loans during tough times, even if his methods were questionable. One day, Selma who was David's Mother in Law, called David in a panic--Ben had been arrested for "loan sharking." His landlord, predictably, served him with a 30-day eviction notice.

With their son still in college, Selma was desperate, fearing they'd lose everything. She begged David to find a business that could provide them with immediate income. David spent an entire day racking his brain for a solution, but nothing materialized. Out of options, he asked Cal if he'd consider selling his retail nut store in San Marino. Cal hesitated, wanting to discuss it with his family before making a decision.

Everyone met at the Garvey Nut House the following Saturday morning. David asked again if they'd sell the store, but Cal refused, saying he wanted to keep it for future security. In a last-ditch attempt, David, out of pure desperation, offered, "What if I trade you half of Jelly Belly?"

Cal and his family immediately accepted, their eyes lighting up. The store was worth, at most, $20,000, including inventory and the cash in the register. It didn't even include real estate. For Cal, it was like trading a cow for a Lamborghini.

Once Ben took over the store, his quirky personality didn't quite mesh with the local clientele. In the window, David had placed a 10-pound jawbreaker as a marketing gimmick, hoping to use it as a pitch to appear on the Dinah Shore Show. But one day, David walked in to find it missing. When he asked Ben what happened, Ben proudly held his suspenders and announced, "Sold it for ten bucks! Pretty good, huh?"

David's heart sank at his father-in-law's pride. He knew how much time and effort had gone into creating that jawbreaker, but Ben thought he was simply making a smart business move. Another time, Ben looked at David and said, "You know, you didn't have to get me a store as nice as this. All I needed was a popcorn machine, and I could've made enough to survive." David couldn't help but feel a mix of amusement and frustration, realizing that Ben had no understanding of the complexities involved in running a successful business.

From the moment Cal became David's partner, Herman Rowland from Herman Goelitz showed clear resentment. Perhaps it was the way Cal appeared on the scene so suddenly or the way his relaxed approach clashed with Herm's control-ling tendencies.

Ben and Selma-Rebecca's Parents

David's willingness to help Ben at such a personal cost demonstrated his character and loyalty. Though he faced challenges from Herm Rowland and the uncertainties of the business world, David chose to prioritize his family. In doing so, he not only provided Ben with a lifeline but also solidified his own legacy of kindness and support during times of crisis, proving himself to be a truly good person despite the sacrifices he had to make.

Life with Cal and Helene

Cal

Helena

Cal was a man who appeared straightforward but carried a quiet complexity. An only child, he lived with a lingering suspicion that he might have been adopted. This wasn't a baseless feeling; one day, he confided in David about a call he'd made to a hospital in St. Louis, where he believed he was born. "They have no record of me," he'd said, a touch of doubt in his voice. It was a mystery he carried, one he never resolved, and David often wondered if Cal ever found peace with this unanswered question.

Cal's parents owned a small nut store on their property in South El Monte, California, where they'd also built a few apartment units. Their entrepreneurial spirit influenced Cal, even though he chose a different path and became a high school teacher. In Monterey Park, California, he taught typing and bookkeeping, subjects that suited his practical, meticulous nature.

One piece of advice Cal stood by was the value of real estate near water. "There's only so much ocean, David," he'd say. "They can't make any more of it." This wisdom drove his investments. His first condominium was a one-bedroom in Redondo Beach, California, and when he moved to a second condo, he rented out the first one. This approach eventually brought him financial security, even though he remained exceedingly frugal. David often joked that when Cal opened his wallet, cobwebs came out.

Despite his wealth, Cal's cautious nature extended to everything, even down to their monthly tradition of lunch meetings. For 20 years, they met at different restaurants, with Cal bringing David his monthly check. Yet, Cal's wallet never saw the light of day. David always paid, but he didn't mind; it had become a comforting ritual between them.

One day, Cal called David on the phone, his voice unusually serious. "I have something of extreme importance to talk to you about," he began. David, curious, replied, "Sure, go ahead, I've got time."

"As you might know, I've just reached the age where I can receive Medicare," Cal explained. "I don't think it's fair that the business pays for your health insurance. I think it's only fair for you to pay for your own policy now." David wasn't surprised by Cal's practicality. By this point, he was well-acquainted with Cal's firm sense of fairness and his frugality.

Helene, Cal's wife, shared a similar practicality, often displaying a no-nonsense attitude that sometimes rubbed people the wrong way. She managed the retail store for their nut business and had a reputation for her cooking, especially her seven-layer guacamole dip, which was a staple at gatherings. David's wife, Rebecca, admired Helene's cooking and tried to replicate her recipes. But each time Rebecca received a recipe, it seemed as if something was missing, as if Helene had deliberately left out a key ingredient, making it hard to recreate her dishes. David wasn't certain if it was intentional, but Rebecca couldn't shake the feeling that Helene preferred to keep some of her culinary secrets to herself.

David's early experiences in the wholesale nut business were memorable. His first wholesale customer was Carson, who owned Carson's Candy at the Farmer's Market in Los Angeles. David drove to the store, carrying a case of walnuts, hoping to secure a sale. Carson was impressed with the nuts' freshness and bought four cases, paying $98 for the lot. David returned to the business feeling accomplished and proudly handed the check to Helene, who was handling the books.

"What did these walnuts cost us?" she asked critically. "Ninety dollars," David replied, expecting a smile of encouragement. Instead, she said, "We didn't make much money on this, did we, Dave?" Her practicality sometimes felt more like criticism, and though it stung, David reminded himself of his father's advice: "Man should learn to compliment more and complain less." He held his tongue, though he wished for a bit more encouragement from Helene.

Working with Cal had its quirks. They sold various items, including large 60-pound bags of bran, and Cal's frugality was ever-present. One day, a forklift punctured a bag of bran, spilling about a pound onto the floor. Cal sighed, "There goes today's profit," highlighting his tendency to see loss even in the smallest mishaps. David appreciated his friend's humor, though he often felt Cal's intense focus on every detail could be challenging.

David seldom took vacations, as his pricing expertise was critical to their business, and he handled most customer interactions. Cal didn't know the product costs and wasn't involved in pricing, so David bore the weight of negotiations. In those days, everything was done manually, and each sale had to be noted by hand.

One incident showcased their differing approaches. David had recently developed a new product, Triple Dipple, a gourmet candy corn with flavors like Neapolitan, Piña Colada, and Strawberry Daiquiri. Known as the creator of Jelly Belly jelly beans, David was excited to launch this innovative candy. Before leaving for a family day at the amusement park, he set up a pallet of Triple Dipple, arranging it in a way that made it look as though it was selling fast, hoping the display would make the product appear popular.

However, when David returned the next day, he saw that Cal had rearranged the display. Always neat and orderly, Cal had stacked the cases into precise rows, unintentionally giving the impression that the product hadn't been touched. David couldn't help but feel that the overly tidy display had taken away from the product's appeal. Triple Dipple never took off as they'd hoped, and David sometimes wondered if Cal's well-intentioned "tidying" had inadvertently jinxed it.

One day, Cal heard a knock on the door at his condo. When he answered, he found two police officers standing outside. "Are you Mr. Lieberman?" one of them asked. Cal confirmed he was. They asked if he knew a woman by name, and Cal nodded, explaining that she was his tenant. The officers informed him that she was operating a house of prostitution out of his condo. Cal was floored. He'd assumed she was in the antique business and hadn't suspected anything unusual. This was just one of those situations in which Cal often found himself, completely caught off guard by the unexpected.

Amid these twists and turns, Cal endured personal tragedies as well. He had two daughters, but one, a kind and loving person, passed away from cancer at a young age. Her death was a devastating blow that forever changed him. The lightheartedness he once had, seemed to fade, and David noticed a sadness settling into his friend. Years later, when Cal himself passed away, David was surprised when Helene informed him that the funeral would be "for family only." After all, David's children had known him as "Uncle Cal" and he'd been like family. Still, David respected Helene's wishes, choosing to hold on to the good memories and let go of his disappointment.

Although Helene's demeanor was often reserved and critical, she was a reliable partner in the business. She ran the retail store with efficiency, and her no-nonsense approach to the business was something David grew to respect over time, even if her manner sometimes felt more like reproach than encouragement. Through the years, they built a mutual respect, their interactions tinged with a formality that became their working norm.

Another important person that helped David and Cal run the business was Bob Mahan. Bob originally worked for Fosselman's Ice Cream in Alhambra, California. As the business was growing, David needed someone to help with all the deliveries. David asked Bob if he wanted to come work with him, and Bob quickly accepted. In all of the hundred's of deliveries that Bob made, he never made one mistake in picking the orders or in delivering the order. They couldn't have asked for a better person to help in the business.

Reflecting on his years with Cal and Helene, David saw their journey as a blend of challenges and fulfillment. Cal's frugal approach had taught him the importance of caution, while Helene's pragmatic nature reminded him to remain resilient. Their lives were interwoven with his own, creating a tapestry of successes, frustrations, and shared moments he carried forward with bittersweet fondness. Their friendship, with all its complexities, was a part of David's story, a story of loyalty, growth, and the profound impact of unlikely partnerships.

Nudie Was One of a Kind

David's deliveries for the health food store on Lankershim Boulevard were routine. It was owned by Dennis Weaver, a proponent of nutrition and well-known for his role as Chester on *Gunsmoke*. Weaver was an early advocate for health and wellness, and his store was well-known among locals. David, who had spent years driving his reliable routes around the San Fernando Valley, had a special strategy for getting around. He was known as "Side Street Man" by his customers because he preferred avoiding the freeways and took the side streets instead, winding his way from Van Nuys to Seal Beach and beyond. David couldn't afford a spare tire in those days, and didn't want to risk getting a flat on the freeway. David also knew that driving the side streets would allow him a view of many potential customers as he passed by them. One day, after making his delivery to Dennis, something unusual caught his eye on his way back.

Just a little after 11:30 a.m., David passed a store he'd driven by countless times without a second glance: *Nudie's*. It was impossible to miss that day, though, because parked outside was a car with horns jutting out from the hood, shining like a beacon in the late morning sunlight. The store was legendary, known for its flashy rhinestone suits and western-inspired flair that graced the biggest names in music and entertainment. But David had never ventured inside. His practical side had always kept him away. Nudie's clothing was famous, and famously expensive, but David was intrigued enough by the unusual sight to stop in.

When he opened the door, David was greeted almost immediately by Nudie Cohn himself. Nudie, a renowned tailor to the stars, known for outfitting Elvis Presley, Glen Campbell, and countless others, was a larger-than-life figure with a keen eye for fashion. As he looked David up and down, Nudie's discerning gaze took in every detail of his visitor's outfit. In less than ten seconds, he gave his assessment: "Son, my clothing is very expensive. I suggest that you go two miles north to Sears where they will have clothing that you can afford."

David, though dressed modestly, wasn't deterred. Instead, he explained that he was preparing for an upcoming appearance on *The Mike Douglas Show*. It would be his second time on the show, and he wanted something different from his usual attire—a wardrobe upgrade that would make an impression. When Nudie heard this, his attitude shifted entirely. Here was a man looking to make a statement, not just buy clothes. Nudie set to work, assembling an outfit that would go down as one of David's most memorable: a pair of custom pants, a shirt, a belt, boots, a mask, a jacket, and a massive ten-gallon hat. The total price? $4,300—an investment in style that David felt was worth every penny.

That outfit, meticulously crafted and emblazoned with the signature sparkle and unique style Nudie was known for, made David feel like he was stepping into a new version of himself. He wore it with pride, debuting it on *The Mike Douglas Show*, where the guest co-host was none other than Henry Winkler, famous for his role as "The Fonz" on *Happy Days*. The experience was surreal, as David had come up with the idea for Jelly Belly jelly beans while watching *Happy Days* years earlier. Meeting Winkler face-to-face felt like a full-circle moment, connecting David's candy legacy to the pop culture he'd grown up watching.

David also wore his Nudie suit for an appearance on *Good Morning New York*. As he stepped out of the studio, he encountered Mayor Ed Koch, who took one look at him and said with a grin, "Nice outfit, cowboy." David, with his ten-gallon hat and rhinestone suit, had clearly made a New York impression.

Years later, David found himself at a candy trade show where he encountered Herm Rowland, who was accompanied by one of the owners of Jolly Rancher candy. Spotting David's distinctive outfit, Herm asked if he could borrow the ten-gallon hat for his friend. David, always generous, agreed on the condition that the hat be returned to him. Unfortunately, a year passed without any sign of the hat, and David began making calls. He reached out to the owner of Jolly Rancher, but was told they didn't have a tracking number for the return. A while later, he followed up again and learned that the hat had supposedly been passed off to a race car driver who would meet Herm at a car show. To this day, David never got his original Nudie ten-gallon hat back. He imagines it as a trophy in some unknown corner of the world, a piece of his story left behind. David would love to one day get his ten-gallon hat back—no questions asked.

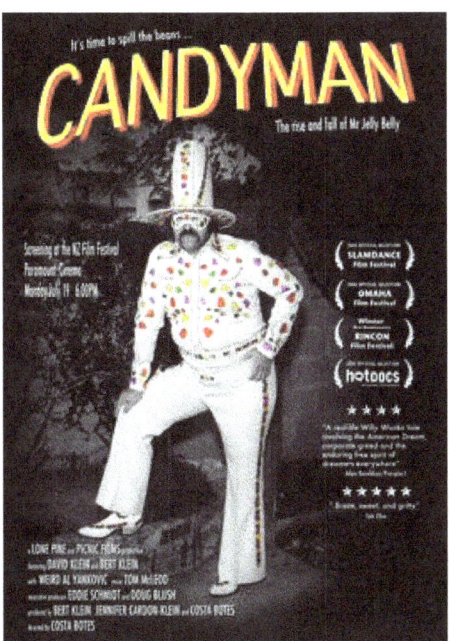

Missing Original 10 gallon hat

David does, however, still have a similar hat, also crafted by Nudie, which he wears with pride when reminiscing about those early days. His son keeps part of the original outfit, a cherished reminder of his father's unforgettable entrance into the world of celebrity fashion. David himself had the pleasure of donning his Nudie suit on multiple television appearances, including five times with Regis Philbin on *A.M. Los Angeles*. The outfit became part of David's public persona, a symbol of his journey through the candy industry and beyond. Nudie's family reached out to David to tell him that he was one of Nudie's favorite customers. His family created a beautiful coffee table book that can be found on Amazon by Jamie Lee Nudie and Mary Lynn Cabrall called Nudie The Rodeo Tailor. They graciously included a picture of me in my outfit in the book.

In 2023, David was invited to appear on *Pawn Stars Do America*. On set, he was greeted by Chumlee, one of the show's stars, who, to David's surprise, was familiar with the Nudie legacy. Chumlee, who also happens to own a candy store across from *Pawn Stars*' Las Vegas location, recognized the Nudie hat and shared some of the history of the tailor's influence on popular culture with the audience. David was thrilled to find that the Nudie legend was still alive and celebrated by a new generation, making the experience memorable for both him and the viewers.

For David, Nudie was a one-of-a-kind artist, a creator who could turn a piece of clothing into an experience, a statement, and a memory. That one encounter in a small shop on Lankershim Boulevard set in motion a series of unforgettable events, connecting David to a legacy of style and personality that was uniquely Nudie.

Money for a Life

David was sitting on the toilet in his bathroom in Van Nuys, the LA Times spread across his lap as he went through his morning routine. The LA Times was a ritual for him, a paper that felt like a friend with its deep, engaging articles. David especially loved the business and sports sections, always looking forward to the columns by Jim Murray, a sports writer who could pull you right into the game. Murray had a sharp wit and a way of writing that stayed with you. David would always remember the line, "Gentlemen, start your coffins," describing the dangers of the Indy 500. Murray's words could take unexpected turns; once, he'd written a column about losing his two best friends, and only at the very end did you realize he was talking about his sight. The man was a genius, David thought.

But that day, a headline in the front section grabbed his attention. David's eyes scanned the page as he read about his former business partner Hal's arrest for arson. It was the late seventies, and Hal, it seemed, had used a Dodgers game as his alibi, attending it while someone he'd hired set fire to his building. Desperate for money, Hal had been looking to cash in on a $2.4 million insurance policy after being sued for putting the name "Remington" on his pens. The fire, however, had spiraled into something terrible. A firefighter, Lynn Hazlett, had died trying to control the flames, and he left behind a pregnant wife and four children. Twenty-four other firefighters had been injured during the three-hour inferno, fueled by photocopying chemicals stored in the building. David felt a sinking feeling as he read on.

Hal was convicted of two counts of mail fraud for filing the insurance claim and one count of arson murder. He received ten years for the murder and six years for the mail fraud, but the judge allowed him to serve both sentences concurrently. Later, on appeal, Hal's arson conviction was overturned; the court ruled the federal government didn't have jurisdiction over the arson charge. Hal's total time served ended up being just three years. David shook his head, barely able to believe it.

Sometime later, David was driving down Ventura Boulevard, thinking back to a term paper he'd written years ago in college about Ventura Boulevard itself. He had meticulously documented each business and the land-use patterns along the boule-vard. David had written that he believed gas stations would someday have restaurants inside them, a vision he was proud of. But his professor, Professor Karlin, hadn't agreed with him. Known for his use of the Socratic method, Professor Karlin would call on students at random to stand up, making them wait in silence for ten minutes or more before he'd finally ask a question. This tactic intimidated students, but it was part of his approach to push them into thinking deeply. Professor Karlin was widely admired and liked for his challenging style, but his skepticism about David's prediction had made him refuse to accept the paper. David had been forced to rewrite the paper on another topic, which was finally accepted.

Then, as he passed Casa De Cadillac, he saw him—Hal, walking along the sidewalk as if nothing had changed. David pulled over, rolling down his window, watching the man he once knew well. The amazing thing about Hal, David always thought, was that he could have been a double for Martin Landau. He looked just the same.

Seeing Hal now, David wondered how different things might have been. If Hal had stuck around and stayed honest, he could have been David's partner in the Jelly Belly business, building something meaningful instead of risking lives. But those choices had been made long ago, and they'd led to vastly different roads.

The next time David would see Hal was at Uncle Earl's funeral, a quiet reminder of all the turns their lives had taken, marked by choices that had set them on paths that could never come together again.

Favorite Customer Stories

In 1974, David and Rebecca were residing in an apartment complex just two blocks from the Santa Anita Racetrack, where some jockeys also lived. At that time, David primarily sold office supplies like Avery labels and Ace staples to dry cleaners and florists, but he was just beginning to venture into the wholesale nut industry. His sole product was shelled walnuts. One day, David entered Prebles Produce Market on Lake in Pasadena to pitch his walnuts. He inquired who the buyer was and was directed to Larry. As David offered Larry new crop walnuts at 98 cents a pound, a customer nearby overheard. Larry quickly pulled David aside and reprimanded him, explaining that discussing prices in front of customers was a serious error. Feeling he had made a blunder, David started to leave very slowly and said "I guess I blew it" but anticipated being called back due to the attractive price. Indeed, Larry, recognizing David's inexperience, decided to give him another shot. This incident became a pivotal learning moment for David; he never again spoke of prices in the presence of customers. Following this, David expanded his product range, and Larry, from 7 a.m. Monday to Saturday, effectively became David's wake-up call, placing daily orders. David fondly remembers Larry referring to "pecan meats" when ordering his typical two cases. Larry's support was crucial in expanding David's business to other Preble locations, significantly sustaining his growing nut venture.

Just a short distance from Prebles, at 560 S. Arroyo Parkway in Pasadena, California, stood a quaint health food store named Granny's Pantry, owned by Gene Scarborough and his wife Evelyn. David, brimming with confidence, walked into Granny's declaring, "I'm in the nut business, and no one can offer you better service or prices." Gene courteously responded that he was content with his current supplier, Dan. David gracefully thanked Gene for his time and asked if he could visit again when in the area, to which Gene agreed warmly.

David made it a routine to stop by Granny's every two or three weeks when he delivered to nearby Prebles. On one such visit, David inquired if there was anything specific that Gene needed which Dan couldn't supply. Gene's eyes lit up as he mentioned needing a bag of raw Spanish peanuts out of the shell. Without discussing the price, David promised to return with the peanuts in two hours.

After driving 20 miles to Torn and Glasser to purchase a 105-pound bag—the heaviest he had ever lifted, which he later suspected caused him a hernia—David returned to Granny's, offering the peanuts at 45 cents a pound, which was 10 cents less than his cost. Despite losing about $10 on the deal, plus the cost of gas and time, David's gesture impressed Gene.

Gene, intrigued by David's pricing, checked his file cabinet and asked if all David's prices were as competitive. Upon hearing an affirmative, Gene assured David all his future business. David began visiting daily, delivering nuts and placing them by the cooler for Gene to inspect, though Gene never felt the need to verify the orders, trusting David implicitly.

David would stock the bulk bins, write his own check from Gene's checkbook, and present it to Gene, his wife, Lois, an employee, or Ralph, his son-in-law, for signing, sometimes for orders exceeding $1,500. Throughout their business relationship, they never questioned David's choices or prices.

In addition to the store, Gene also manufactured Granny's Laundry Detergent in a shed at the back, eventually turning it into a successful venture.

David recalls visiting Ralph and Margo Kidushim's produce store in La Cañada, California, on a bustling Friday afternoon. The affluent area was reflected in the store's atmosphere, with customers streaming in to buy produce for their weekend meals. As Ralph and Margo tended to the steady flow of customers, David patiently waited for about 20 minutes. During this time, he walked around the store and noticed they didn't carry any nut products.

When the store finally cleared, David introduced himself, saying, "I'm in the nut business and can offer you tremendous prices on a product that doesn't spoil in just a few days like produce." Ralph and Margo were immediately intrigued and asked about his pricing. David quoted 98 cents a pound for walnuts out of the shell, explaining that they could easily double their money. They agreed to bring in a case, which sold out in less than a day. This marked the beginning of a lifelong friendship and business relationship that remains strong to this day.

Margo later became a television celebrity and food expert featured on ABC News. When Ralph and Margo opened a new store called Sunshine Produce in Pasadena, David went above and beyond, supplying them at cost plus 5%. He felt that supporting their business in this way not only demonstrated kindness but also fostered a solid foundation for future orders. The grand opening of Sunshine Produce took place on a Saturday, and David set up a booth inside the store to sell Jelly Belly Jelly Beans at $2.00 per pound. Margo's mother was David's very first customer for Jelly Bellies in this location.

Although Ralph was initially skeptical about Jelly Bellies, it became an ongoing joke between him and David. Later, when Margo's mother was living in an assisted living facility, David brought her to his factory and presented her with her favorite treat—Sunkist Fruit Wafers—further cementing the personal and heartfelt bond between them.

Wally Amos gained worldwide fame as the pioneer of the chocolate chip cookie business. However, what many may not know is that before his rise to cookie stardom, he worked at the William Morris Agency, representing legendary artists such as The Temptations and Marvin Gaye, and even signing Simon & Garfunkel.

David boldly walked into Wally's cookie shop one day and confidently said, "I want your business." David promised Wally exceptional service and delivered the finest pecans Wally had ever seen. Recognizing Wally's business acumen, David offered him an equal partnership in his Jelly Belly company. Wally graciously declined, saying, "Dave, I'm not a jelly bean man; I'm a cookie man, but I appreciate the opportunity."

Later, David, Wally Amos, and Irv Robbins of Baskin-Robbins shared a stage at a USC entrepreneurship class. It was a memorable moment, showcasing three unique entrepreneurs who had each left a distinct mark on the world of business.

When David was operating in South El Monte, California, he received a call from a young man named Steve Corri, who wanted to buy nuts wholesale. At first, David was hesitant to sell to Steve because he was fiercely competing with one of David's established customers, Sam. Steve, who arrived at their first meeting with green hair due to his involvement in a rock band, was a talented musician. Despite Steve's persistence, David repeatedly told him, "We have all the customers we need right now."

The turning point came when Steve called David one day, and the sound of his daughter crying could be heard in the background. David asked, "Are you feeding her enough food?" Steve replied, "Yes, when I have the money." Touched by Steve's situation, David told him to come down to meet him.

Sam, one of David's loyal customers, was struggling, and David saw an opportunity to help both Sam and Steve. David made it clear that the only way he would sell to Steve was if Steve bought Sam's accounts. Steve agreed and paid Sam $5,000 in installments to take over his business. This arrangement saved Sam from financial ruin, and to this day, Sam remains grateful to David for his support.

David and Cal started supplying Steve with products, and over time, Steve earned his place in the business, eventually owning one-third of the wholesale nut operation. Steve took on numerous responsibilities, arriving early and dedicating himself fully to the business. In 1990, David and Cal decided to hand over the entire business to Steve for $1. The company was generating approximately $5.5 million annually, but Cal was ready to retire, and David wanted to focus on other ventures. For the deal to go through, Steve made several commitments. Once he took over, he worked tirelessly, seven days a week, often sleeping in the warehouse because he was too exhausted to go home.

Steve had learned customer relations by observing David closely for 13 years. However, David felt regret about the challenges Steve faced when the Jelly Belly Candy Company pressured him not to sell David's new jelly beans after his 20-year non-compete ended. Steve ultimately reported this coercion to the Department of Justice's Antitrust Division, but David remains disappointed that no action was taken against Herm Rowland and his company. Without Steve's business, David's comeback in the jelly bean industry was thwarted.

Steve passed away a few years ago, and David believes his death was linked to the toxic fumes emitted by a neighboring business in South El Monte that manufactured church pews. The chemicals used in the process polluted the parking area, and David vividly recalls Steve arguing with the business owner over the unbearable smell. The fumes were horrific, and David will always remember Steve's dedication, resilience, and the challenges he faced.

David first met Ed Ringle at a nut and candy store in Van Nuys, part of the San Fernando Valley, that was run by Ed's mom, Hilda, and his brother, Dave. They quickly became some of David's favorite customers. Every week, they would place their orders with David's mom, who used a special phone line to relay the orders to David, saving costs during a time when phone calls were charged by the minute, unlike today's unlimited calling plans. Hilda and Dave had a wonderful attitude about life and a genuine love for their business, making them a joy to work with.

One day, during a routine delivery, David met Ed, who arrived wearing sunglasses perched on his head. David found Ed fascinating—full of ideas and energy. At that time, in late 1975, David was in the early stages of developing his line of gourmet jelly beans, which would later become Jelly Bellies. When David mentioned this to Ed, Ed scoffed at the idea, expressing doubt about its potential. Ed even reiterated his skepticism years later in David's documentary. Undeterred, David responded, "Well, give me a better idea." Ed shared that he owned property in Agoura Hills and planned to sell

Christmas trees there during the holidays, complete with live reindeer. David was impressed by the creativity of the concept but remained confident in his jelly bean venture. At that time, only a handful of people supported David's idea, including Rebecca.

A year or so later, Ed built a store modeled after Hadley's Orchard in Cabazon, California, a place he greatly admired. He bought nuts from Garvey and even purchased a truck from David after David upgraded to a larger vehicle. Ed's entrepreneurial spirit didn't stop there. One day, he walked into David and Cal's office with a bold plan to build a casino in Beatty, Nevada—a town David had never heard of. Ed asked if they wanted to invest, but after Ed left, Cal remarked that Ed didn't know the first thing about running a casino and doubted the venture would succeed.

Despite the skepticism, Ed opened the Stagecoach Casino in Beatty. He also built a large gas station across from the casino, a Motel 6, and even started working on a Steampunk Casino along with several townhouses and other projects in the area. Beyond Beatty, Ed expanded his ventures, building Ringle's Resort in Costa Rica and EddieWorld in Yermo, California. EddieWorld is a magical store located between Los Angeles and Las Vegas, and it's worth visiting—not least for the men's restroom, the store features a piece of the Lakers' basketball court on display.

Beatty, nestled between Las Vegas and Reno, became another cornerstone of Ed's accomplishments. David remains in contact with Ed to this day and has immense respect for everything he has achieved, marveling at his creativity and determination in turning ambitious ideas into reality.

Richard Ross called David one day, determined to convince him that he had the energy and drive to become a successful distributor of Jelly Belly Jelly Beans. At just 16 years old, Richard's confidence was impressive, and he expressed his plan to sell Jelly Bellies both in his mother's gift shop and wholesale across a four-state area centered around Kentucky. Despite his youth, David believed in Richard's potential and gave him an extraordinary opportunity that most would hesitate to offer someone so young.

Years later, David visited Richard's thriving business, which had grown into a global distribution operation serving some of the biggest companies in the world. As David prepared to leave Richard's office, he stood below the second-floor atrium while Richard looked down from above. David called out, "Nice to see that you're doing so well." Richard replied, "None of this would have been possible if not for you."

Richard's words deeply moved David. While few people in the world have shown David the admiration and gratitude he deserves for his guidance, help, and goodwill,

Richard's heartfelt acknowledgment has always stood out and continues to warm David's heart.

Tom King was one of David's wholesale customers and owned a store located just five blocks from the beach in the south bay area. One day, Tom called David, distraught. His landlords, Frank and Mary, had drastically increased the rent after Tom had recently purchased their business. David knew the store well, having visited frequently because Cal and his wife lived nearby.

When David first introduced Jelly Bellies to Frank, David was selling nuts to him. Like many of David's nut customers, Frank balked at the $2.00 per pound price of the Jelly Bellies, especially since he was accustomed to buying mini jelly beans at just 60 cents per pound. Later, when Tom took over the business, he sought David's advice, saying, "What should I do?"

Without hesitation, David asked, "If you had to pick one item in your store that you're known for, what would it be?" Tom instantly replied, "Chocolate Graham Crackers." David advised Tom to leave the store location as quickly as possible, not renew the lease, and instead focus exclusively on wholesaling his Chocolate Graham Crackers. David confidently predicted that within a year, Tom would be selling them to Starbucks.

At the time, Tom was enrolled in a program at USC's entrepreneur school. He presented the idea of selling only Chocolate Graham Crackers to his professor, who dismissed it, saying, "If Nabisco thought Chocolate Graham Crackers were a good product, they'd already be making them." Thankfully, Tom ignored that advice. To bolster Tom's confidence, David loaned him a handmade red and purple cape created by Rebecca for David's media appearances. David humorously told Tom never to wash the cape, warning that doing so would remove its magical powers.

Many years later, after Tom achieved tremendous success, David called to order some of his Chocolate Graham Crackers—insisting on paying with a credit card. When the crackers arrived, David immediately noticed something was off. He called Tom and said, "There's carob mixed in with the chocolate." Tom asked for the batch number, checked the product from that batch, and confirmed David's observation. That single error could have derailed Tom's business, but he resolved the issue swiftly.

Tom went on to become a major player in the candy industry, with his Chocolate Graham Crackers earning widespread acclaim. Eventually, Tom sold his business for a significant sum. When David heard about the sale, he called Tom and quipped, "It looks like you no longer need the powers of the cape." True to his word, Tom returned the cape, which David still keeps, waiting for its next assignment.

One of David's customers was Dan Volland, the manager of a health food store called Alpha Nutrition, located along Ventura Boulevard in Studio City. David and Dan hit it off immediately, sharing a mutual understanding and appreciation for the business. A unique aspect of their relationship was that when the store owner occasionally forgot to leave a check for David's nut deliveries, Dan would pay him in Champion Juicers at cost. David would then sell these juicers to other health food stores, such as Granny's Pantry and Bill White's.

Next door to Alpha Nutrition was a specialized gift shop. Dan left Alpha Nutrition to form a partnership with Sandy Gooch. When Sandy set out to revolutionize the health food industry, she approached Dan to partner with her. Together, Sandy and Dan transformed the industry, creating a list of products that became "Gooch Approved." David supplied a significant portion of their inventory, including nuts, Celestial Tea, and Panda Licorice. Recognizing his expertise, they invited David to serve on their board of directors. While honored, David eventually had to resign due to a potential conflict with another major customer, Quin's Nutrition, which was also one of his largest accounts.

Sandy and Dan's business expanded to 8–9 stores before they sold it in 1993 for $56 million to Whole Foods, which was later acquired by Amazon. Tragically, Dan passed away, and David always suspected his death was linked to his exposure to Agent Orange during his time serving in the Army in Vietnam.

Another connection David made at Alpha Nutrition was with Rich Arcaris, a coworker of Dan's. One day, David called Rich for help with a major problem. David had signed a contract for 50,000 pounds of pecans, but the market shifted due to supply and demand. Famous Amos, one of David's clients for pecans, accepted a competitor's lower price, leaving David stuck with the inventory. David offered Rich the pecans at his exact cost, and Rich managed to sell most of them by putting them on sale at cost, saving David from a financial disaster.

Rich later became part of a successful natural food store in Utah called Kathy's Ranch Market. Interestingly, when David first met Rich at Alpha, he offered him half interest or 25% interest in Jelly Belly for $1,000 depending on who's version you hear—a missed opportunity that remains a fascinating footnote. David and Rich still keep in touch to this day.

What David remembers about Curtis is visiting his store in Orange, California, which had the same upscale feel as Gelson's Market, a well-known market chain in the state. Curtis and his dad Mickey had a thoughtful tradition: every Christmas, they gifted everyone at Garvey with stunning red poinsettias. The story of how David acquired Curtis's account is an interesting one. At the time, Curtis was being supplied with nuts by another of David's customers, Charlie. David purchased the rights to Curtis's account from Charlie for a couple of thousand dollars and then supplied Curtis for years afterward.

Charlie himself was a fascinating character. He had been buying almonds from Berrenda Mesa Farms and owed them $30,000. Despite this debt, Charlie called in an order for another $10,000 worth of almonds. When he arrived to pick them up, the farm confronted him, saying they needed payment before supplying more. Charlie, ever the quick thinker, replied, "I have a solution." Expecting a check, they were stunned when he added, "Just increase my credit line." It was one of the funniest moments David recalls in his 60 years of business. Unsurprisingly, Charlie didn't get the almonds. Charlie was extremely personable and one of the friendliest people David had ever known. Tragically, his store was closed for months, and when he tried to reopen it, he discovered the building had burned down. The fire department had somehow acquired it and used it for fire training exercises.

Curtis, however, had complete trust in David. One day, he told David, "I want one case of everything new that you have. You don't need my approval—just always bring me anything new." Inspired by this, David began asking all his customers for similar permission. Many agreed, which significantly boosted his business since customers weren't always present when David delivered orders to showcase new products. As a result, David constantly sought out innovative items, bringing in products like Turkish Apricots, Banana Chips, Sesame Sticks, Japanese crackers (marketed as Fun Mix), a pecan-flavored snack made from wheat germ, Corn Nuts, Panda Licorice, Bowlby Bits, and dozens of others. David was often the first to import these products into the U.S.

One standout memory was the American demand for Haribo gummy bears. David discovered another brand, Katjes, whose gummy bears he preferred. He tracked down their broker, RJ Allen, and negotiated a deal to import a truckload—40,000 pounds—for $42,000. Cal's reaction upon seeing the bill was priceless; he thought David had lost his mind. But after tasting the gummy bears, Cal declared, "These are better than Haribo." Not only were the Katjes gummy bears 45 cents cheaper per pound, but David also convinced every customer to switch brands. Katjes quickly became a major name in California, thanks to David's efforts. On top of that, David negotiated favorable terms, allowing him 60 days to pay the bill while still securing a 2% discount.

Curtis's trust and openness to new products not only strengthened his relationship with David but also drove innovation and success across David's entire business.

One day, David was standing in the parking lot of Garvey Nut House in Vernon, California, around 1 p.m. or so, when a car pulled up and Sandy Licht stepped out. Sandy greeted David with an air of excitement and said, "You're never going to believe what I have here." Intrigued, David replied, "Three guesses?" but couldn't figure it out.

Sandy revealed that he had just returned from a trip to England, where he had purchased the rights to the name and formula for Walnettos from the Cadbury Candy Company. Cadbury had acquired Walnettos from Peter Paul Candies, who had originally bought it from J.N. Collins, the inventor of the candy in 1919. Cadbury had decided to discontinue the product because it wasn't generating enough business, so they sold it to Sandy.

Walnettos had gained a level of fame thanks to its connection with the popular TV show Laugh-In, which aired from 1968 to 1973. Arte Johnson's recurring character, a dirty old man, made the phrase "Wanna Walnetto?" a memorable catchphrase.

David congratulated Sandy, who then showed him the receipt for the purchase. David was impressed by the significant amount Sandy had paid for the rights. What struck David even more was a connection from five years earlier when he had been in the office of Arnold Gendel and was considering buying that very trademark—a memory that tied into the story of Walnettos.

David's first recollection of Ken Finley was when he walked into a cheese store that Ken owned in the prestigious Arcadia Mall on Baldwin Avenue. The mall was two stories, and Ken's shop was located on the first floor, right next to the Arcadia Horse Race Track, which, incidentally, served the best French Dip sandwiches David had ever tasted. One December day, David walked into the store and found Ken handing out samples of smoked Gouda cheese.

At the time, Jelly Belly Jelly Beans had only been on the market for about three months. David introduced himself to Ken and showed him the Jelly Bellies, explaining that Ken's cost would be $1.00 per pound. He pointed out that there were 400 beans to a pound, and Ken could sell them for at least $2.00 per pound. David emphasized that there was no minimum order but noted that the beans didn't come assorted. To stock all eight flavors, Ken would need to buy eight 30-pound cases, requiring a $240 investment—a considerable amount of money back then. Ken carefully considered the proposal but ultimately said, "I'm going to have to pass on that."

Every time David visited the Arcadia Mall, he would stop by The Helen Grace store to check on their Jelly Belly supply, then head over to Ken's shop and ask, "Are you ready to order Jelly Bellies yet?" Determined to persuade him, David suggested that Ken create an entire candy department in his store, offering to supply it himself. Eventually, David's persistence paid off, and Ken agreed. Ken would often visit Garvey Nut with a helper, usually a man named Louie, to pick up stock.

One memorable coincidence occurred when David was at home in Glendora, retrieving his mail. Across the street, he spotted Ken and Louie in a car, searching for an address. They each looked at each other and said in unison "I know you!" Recognizing each other immediately, David waved them over and invited them into his home, where he made them pastrami sandwiches on rye. During the visit, they discovered they shared the exact same birthday, further cementing their bond.

When Ken would go to Garvey Nut to stock up on inventory, David trusted him completely. He handed Ken a blue ready-form invoice book and let him write out his own invoices. David never felt the need to check them, as he knew Ken was honest and reliable. Their relationship was built on trust and mutual respect, which David always cherished.

Gingham Gardens was an upscale gift store originally located on Wilshire Boulevard in California before later moving to Larchmont Avenue. Across the street from its original location was W&J Sloane, where David's father, Louis, worked as the top furniture salesman for eight consecutive years. Gingham Gardens was owned by a charming couple, Nate and Beverly Blitzer, who also ran a private high-end clothing com-pany. Their business was so renowned that they produced the top Barbara Streisand made famous.

One day, Suzy Kalter—later known as Suzy Gershman—visited Gingham Gardens. Suzy was a celebrated American writer and the author of sixteen Born to Shop travel guides over a span of 25 years, selling more than 4 million copies. She and her husband formed a remarkable power couple; her husband managed numerous legendary artists, including Looking Glass (famous for "Brandy", James Taylor, Neil Diamond, Elton John, The Doors, and Jefferson Airplane. He also worked as a publicist for stars like Woody Allen, Dick Cavett, Lionel Richie, Mel Tormé, and Joan Rivers.

During her visit, Suzy asked Nate and Beverly what was new and popular in the store. They enthusiastically replied, "The hottest item we have in here are Jelly Belly Jelly Beans. We can't keep them in stock." Intrigued, Suzy took down David's information and called him that same day. On the call, she said, "I heard about your product from Beverly and Nate. How would you like to meet me tomorrow morning at 10 a.m.? I'll write you up for People Magazine—it's exactly the kind of story that gets approved easily." True to her word, Suzy arrived the next day, impeccably dressed in one of the most stunning outfits David had ever seen.

The resulting article appeared in People Magazine, with O.J. Simpson on the cover. It included a now-iconic photo of David in a bathtub filled with Jelly Belly Jelly Beans, his chest bare. To prepare for the shoot, David rented a prop bathtub from a Hollywood store that supplied the film industry. He transported it in his box truck to Garvey Nut, where it stayed until the People Magazine photographer arrived later that week. When the photographer was ready, David stepped into the tub wearing shorts, and the beans were poured in around him. The article had a transformative effect, turning Jelly Belly Jelly Beans into a household name.

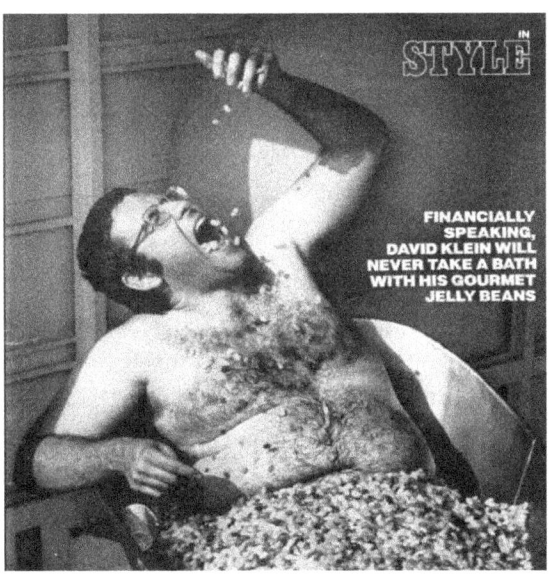

*David in a tub of beans *People Magazine**

David has always appreciated the contributions of Nate, Beverly, and Suzy to the success of Jelly Bellies. In 2012, he called Suzy to thank her again and offered to visit her the next day. Though Suzy was delighted to hear from him, she regretfully explained that she was very ill and couldn't meet. Sadly, it was their last conversation.

David remains in contact with Nate and Beverly's son, Ron Blitzer, who is a highly accomplished businessman with a passion for environmental issues. Among his achievements, Ron developed the soft-serve yogurt program seen in A&PM stores nationwide. During one conversation, David asked Ron about his parents, and Ron shared a story that perfectly captured their kindness. When Nate would run into Ron's customers he would thank them for doing business with his son—a reflection of the family's generosity and thoughtfulness.

David first connected with Chris Segawa through Chris's cousin, Russell, who, along with his wife Cynthia, were early and enthusiastic supporters of Sandy Candy. Russell and Cynthia referred over 10 people to the business and frequently collaborated with David, including working together at street fairs, where David joined their family dozens of times to help at the events.

Both Chris and Russell were entrepreneurial and ambitious, showing a deep passion for business and a willingness to put in long hours. They were also involved in the early stages of the POGs craze, a collectible phenomenon that started in Hawaii. Chris owned a hair salon called Asian Arts in the South Bay area and had dabbled in acting, landing roles, including one in a casino. Despite the distance, Chris often visited David's factory in Covina, placing orders by phone while Russell picked the flavors in person from David's selection of over 90 options. Chris frequently made late-night trips to pick up orders, showcasing his dedication to his business.

An unforgettable moment occurred when Chris's sister-in-law, Terry, visited Garvey in Vernon. As she stepped out of her car, David greeted her by saying, "You're pregnant." Unknown to David, Terry had just come from an OB appointment and hadn't shared the news with anyone, not even her husband. Her astonished reaction, coupled with David's self-proclaimed "mystical abilities," left a lasting impression. Terry was also a business-minded individual, running a women's co-op to organize group purchases of nuts and dried fruits.

Chris's wife later achieved notable success, being elected Mayor of her hometown, a reflection of their family's community involvement and leadership. Throughout the years, Chris has remained a steadfast friend and supporter of every business venture

David has pursued. Beyond their business dealings, Chris visited David's office monthly to give him haircuts, further deepening their personal connection.

The first time David met Allen Mitchell was at a trade show held at the Ambassador Hotel in Los Angeles, the same site as the famous Cocoanut Grove nightclub and, tragically, the location where Bobby Kennedy was assassinated. Coincidentally, Rebecca's cousin Robert, a private detective, was also at the hotel that day. David heard Robert quietly whisper, "Hey, come over," and went to see him, surprised to find him there. When David asked why he was at the trade show, Robert replied, "I'm working as a private investigator."

Allen Mitchell, now in his 92nd year of life, still jokingly claims that David was wearing a diaper the first time they met. Though David has no memory of such a costume and would have readily admitted it if true, both Allen and his late wife Dorothy insist it happened. Outnumbered, David concedes that it might have been the case. However, the only costume David distinctly remembers wearing was that of a cocktail waitress, which he donned to promote his whiskey-flavored, non-alcoholic hard candy called On The Rocks.

Over the years, David has cherished his conversations with Allen, who was a candy distributor with a sharp eye for spotting the next big candy or cookie trend. Allen dealt in novelty items such as candy-filled sharks, jelly cups, and honey sesame cookies from Japan. David always enjoyed how Allen answered the phone with a cheerful "Mitchell here," recognizing David by his caller ID.

Allen grew up in Highland Park, California, where his father owned a supermarket. One day, during a conversation, David blurted out, "Was your dad's supermarket on 54th Street?" To Allen's astonishment, the answer was yes. When Allen asked how David knew, David could only reply, "I have no idea how I knew, I just felt that it was there."

Allen was also good friends with Dave Gold, the founder of the 99 Cents Only Stores. What stands out most about Allen is his incredibly positive attitude, which David believes has been a key factor in his longevity. David deeply values the friendship and fond memories he shares with Allen, whose optimism and energy have left a lasting impression.

David's relationships were just as impactful as his business ventures. He built a network of loyal partners and friends, many of whom shared stories of trust, kindness, and the occasional hilarious moment. From sharing pastrami sandwiches with Ken Finley in his home to helping a struggling friend shift their entire business focus, David's interactions reflect his commitment to lifting others up.

If you enjoyed this book, please consider leaving a review on the site where you purchased it. Your feedback can make a big difference, helping others discover the story and David Klein's mission to pay off The Jelly Belly Candy Company and be financially free from them. If you know a friend who loves candy or has an interest in business, this book could be the perfect gift! Sharing the story with others who might appreciate it is a wonderful way to support David's journey. Thank you for helping spread the word!

We're Coming to Town and Not Leaving

David was basking in the radiant glow of success, his heart swelling with pride as he reflected on his journey with the famous Jelly Belly jelly beans. These tiny, colorful treats had become a global sensation, and to David, they were more than just a product; they felt like a child he had nurtured from conception to success. He was not only a proud father to his two children but also to this sweet invention that had brought joy to so many.

Every moment of hard work and late nights had been worth it. Jelly Belly jelly beans were a household name, loved by people of all ages. David's mother was his biggest cheerleader, sharing his jelly beans with friends and especially with her hairdresser. To make it easier for her, David prepared one-pound bags, allowing her to hand them out effortlessly. The joy he felt seeing his parents enjoy his success was a reward in itself.

When *People Magazine* reached out to feature his story, David seized the opportunity with both hands. He rented a truck and an old-fashioned bathtub, determined to create a memorable photo shoot. On that hot summer day with temperatures over 100, he donned only bathing shorts and filled the tub with Jelly Belly jelly beans, a playful and whimsical choice that embodied his personality. The jelly beans clung to him, getting stuck in his chest hair and between his toes, but he was having the time of his life.

David was grateful to his friend Ron Blitzer, whose parents owned a high-class gift shop called Gingham Gardens on Wilshire Boulevard in Beverly Hills. Ron's parents had shared David's story with a writer named Suzy Kalter (later Gershan), who had helped elevate the visibility of Jelly Belly. Gingham Gardens was one of the original retailers of Jelly Belly, and Suzy brought her young daughter to the Fosselman location, where they took photos together by the Jelly Belly stand. The resulting article in *People Magazine* launched David's jelly beans into another stratosphere of popularity, captivating readers nationwide.

However, the success also stirred unrest within David's contract manufacturer, Herm Rowland. Known for his showmanship, David loved to create buzz and excitement, thinking outside the box—far beyond the realm of conventional marketing. But when that magazine cover hit the stands, it sparked a wave of conversation. Herm was not amused.

"Dave just blew the whole product by posing naked in a bathtub of beans," Herm told his sales manager, although David had, of course, been wearing bathing shorts—barely visible in the photo. The fallout was swift; Herm cut David's production immediately and redirected efforts to sell their old product, candy corn, which was produced on the same equipment. David later learned this and Herm had never explained the sudden halt in production, leaving him in the dark and desperate.

As orders poured in from stores eager to stock Jelly Belly, David found himself in a precarious situation. He placed order after order with Herm, but they never materialized. Stores were furious, inundating him with calls, demanding the jelly beans they had promised to their customers.

In this tumultuous period, David had a candy broker named Beverly Thomas who turned in a hefty order for $30,000 worth of Jelly Bellies to sell to Ralph's Supermarket. However, David wanted to maintain the classy gourmet image of Jelly Bellies and politely declined the order. Beverly, unfazed, responded, "Okay, no problem, I'll create my own."

Taking matters into her own hands, she contacted Just Born candy company, one of the few manufacturers with capacity on their mogul—a vital piece of equipment for making jelly beans, notoriously expensive and hard to come by. Beverly launched her own line of mini jelly beans called Teeny Beanie, a name David found amusing. To add insult to injury, she sold them to one of David's accounts, Knott's Berry Farm.

When David visited Knott's Berry Farm shortly after their first order of Teeny Beanies, he discovered they were still using the same jar that said "Jelly Belly." The sight left him with mixed emotions but ultimately determined to stay focused on his business.

The tension mounted when David received an ominous call from Herm. "I'm coming to town," Herm announced.

"Great! I'll pick you up at the airport. What airport are you flying into?" David replied, hoping for a friendly visit.

"Dave, it's not that kind of meeting," Herm replied, a chill settling in.

"What kind of meeting is this?" David asked, confusion turning into dread.

"I'm coming to town to buy your trademark, and I'm not leaving until I do," Herm declared, a forcefulness that David had never encountered before.

As Herm arrived, accompanied by his sales manager and accountant—David and his business partner Cal Lieberman sat across the table, acutely aware of the weight of the meeting. In the back of his mind, David recalled the whispers he had heard about a

"Plan B" if he refused to sell: Herm would cut him off from any future manufacturing, planning to launch a competing product under his own name.

The realization made David feel sick. He understood that there were few manufacturers who would offer production time on their moguls. Even if he found a new manufacturer, the tooling for molds to create a mini jelly bean would take months to develop. The walls were closing in. Herm knew all of David's customers, having drop-shipped orders directly to them, leaving David with limited options.

In that moment of desperation, David recognized he had no choice but to relinquish his rights, or face losing everything he had built. Herm bluntly acknowledged that David could sue him, but warned that the legal battle would drain David's resources, leaving him broke in the end.

On the way to sign the contract, David gathered the courage to ask, "What would you have done if I hadn't signed?" David wanted to hear it directly from Herm.

Herm's response confirmed it. "I would have cut you off and renamed the product under my own name." To prove his point, he showed David a piece of paper with the new name written down.

That day marked the beginning of a dark chapter in David's life. He returned home, burdened by the weight of his decision, and began a 30-year journey into depression. Despite his internal struggle, he wore a smile for the world, always striving to help others find their own paths to success.

In the contract with Herm, an important detail was the structured payment plan that would continue for two decades. Herm agreed to pay David and Cal up to $20,000 per month, depending on the previous month's sales. This payment was set to continue for 20 years, split evenly between David and Cal. A crucial clause in the contract stated that if Herm missed a payment for two consecutive months, the trademark would revert back to David and Cal. This nearly became a reality during the third year. Cal, noticing they hadn't been paid for the last 50 days, called Herm's accountant to get an explanation. The accountant, who had only recently taken on this position, apologized and sent the check immediately, averting a potential crisis.

In the midst of this turmoil, David worked with his daughter Roxy to bring her creation to life: a make-your-own candy art you can eat. Inspired by a sand art bottle filled with beautifully layered sand from Knott's Berry Farm, this simple moment ignited a new idea they called Sandy Candy.

Determined to turn this passion into a new venture, David opened a small factory to produce Sandy Candy. Yet, despite his accomplishments, Joy was hard to find for David.

Licorice

.

David's earliest memory of licorice stretches back to a summer day at Knott's Berry Farm when he was just six years old. Among the candy-packed shelves, he spotted a modest package of black licorice. The strong, slightly bitter flavor was unlike anything he'd ever tasted, yet he immediately fell in love with it. Unusual for a child, as most kids might find black licorice too intense or "grown-up," but David's taste buds welcomed its distinctive taste. This early experience planted a seed that would grow into a lifelong fascination and journey with licorice.

His affection for licorice only deepened in the years that followed. A short walk from his house in Van Nuys, a small drugstore carried a brand with a camel on the packaging, produced by YNS Candy Company. Little did he know that this very brand would eventually be bought by Hershey's and evolve into the well-known Twizzler line.

As David grew older, he realized there was a distinct divide among licorice lovers. There seemed to be two types of people in the world: those on the West Coast who swore by Red Vines and those on the East Coast who were devoted to Twizzlers. Once someone committed to a brand, they rarely strayed. This preference became almost tribal, with passionate followers on each side.

It wasn't until 1979 that David's passion turned entrepreneurial. He was working with a company that had just received a significant order—1,000 pounds of Red Vines licorice, neatly packed in 20-pound cases, from the American Licorice Company. As he inspected the shipment, a thought struck him: Why not create a sour version of this popular treat? Sour candy had been gaining traction, and he believed that adding a sour twist to licorice could be a hit.

Within three days, David and his team perfected the recipe. They placed 120 pieces of sour red licorice, all standing upright, in clear tubs with a small plastic tong for easy access. This new product was aptly named "I Can't Believe It's So Sour." Although they experimented with different colored licorice, black licorice was notably absent from their selection. After some experimentation, they discovered that black licorice didn't pair well with a sour flavor and that the demand for red licorice far outweighed that of its darker counterpart. Moreover, there were emerging health concerns regarding black licorice, including its potential to lower potassium levels in the body.

The sour licorice debuted in liquor stores, which held a special significance for David. From the ages of six to thirteen, he worked in a liquor store, gaining his first experiences in the world of retail. As fate would have it, one of their first distributors was a close connection—his friend's girlfriend. She began selling their product to liquor stores, creating a thriving business in the process.

The next major step for "I Can't Believe It's So Sour" was Price Club, the precursor to today's Costco. Founded by the visionary Sol Price, Price Club was a beacon of wholesale innovation. Despite its success, however, David learned of a heartbreaking family dispute that eventually led Sol Price to part ways with his son. Price Club placed a $10,000 order for the sour licorice, which became a staple on their shelves, and reorders poured in. So much so that American Licorice sent one of their brokers to investigate why David was ordering such high volumes.

But the excitement of success was short-lived. During one of his visits to Price Club, David discovered a competitor's sour licorice displayed at a considerably lower price point. The rival product was made by Kenny's Licorice for a company called Simon Home Foods, and it quickly gained traction. This competitive pricing posed a significant threat to David's business, eventually cutting into their sales and diminishing the once-promising future of "I Can't Believe It's So Sour."

Despite the setback, David's passion for licorice never wavered. One of his favorite varieties was chocolate licorice, a rare delicacy that had been produced by the American Licorice Company. When Daid opened a retail store called The Jelly Belly in Studio City, California, he stocked 5 ½-inch chocolate licorice sticks. This particular product attracted loyal patrons, including some with notable names. One of David's most memorable customers was Frank Sinatra, who regularly ordered the chocolate licorice, shipped directly to his Palm Springs residence.

David's story with licorice wasn't merely about a love for the taste; it was about discovery, passion, and the relentless pursuit of new possibilities within the candy world. From that first bite at Knott's Berry Farm to stocking shelves with the chocolate licorice favored by Ol' Blue Eyes himself, David's life with licorice was as varied and vibrant as the candy itself.

Bernie Squeals

David Klein's journey in the candy industry has been filled with unexpected turns, challenges, and victories. Known as the creator of Jelly Belly jelly beans, he was eager to tell his story in his own words. That chance finally came with the documentary *Candyman: The David Klein Story*, which chronicles his life, his unique candy creations, and his passion for the industry. The film, available on YouTube, gave David a platform to share his story with the world. But promoting it came with challenges he hadn't anticipated.

When the documentary was released, David reached out to Bernie Pacyniak, the Editor-in-Chief of *Candy Industry Magazine*, in hopes of generating some buzz. David asked Bernie if he knew who he was, to which Bernie replied, "Of course I do." David then asked why, given his contributions to the industry, he'd never been interviewed by the magazine. Bernie responded, "Well, it's time that I do."

David sent Bernie a rare book about Bernie's own company, along with an advance copy of the *Candyman* documentary to help prepare for the interview. A month later, when David called Bernie to confirm, he was taken aback by Bernie's response: "There's not going to be any interview."

Shocked, David asked Bernie why he'd changed his mind. Bernie explained that Herm Rowland, the owner of Jelly Belly Candy Company (formerly Herman Goelitz), had told him not to publish the interview. Although Herm wasn't Bernie's direct boss, *Candy Industry Magazine* depended heavily on ad revenue, and Herm was one of their largest advertisers. David understood Bernie's difficult position, but he felt it crossed an ethical line. He believed journalism should have a code of ethics, and Bernie's decision to pull the interview due to outside pressure seemed unfair. Even to this day, David has never been featured in *Candy Industry Magazine* as the inventor of Jelly Belly jelly beans.

The timing was especially unfortunate, as the documentary was about to debut at the Slamdance Film Festival in Park City, Utah. The publicity from the magazine interview would have been a significant boost. Nevertheless, David focused on the festival screening and hoped it would help bring attention to his story. His time in Park City turned out to be full of memorable moments and amusing encounters.

Upon arriving in the charming mountain town, David found it tough to adjust to the 7,000-foot altitude, which left him short of breath for much of his ten-day stay. Excited to show his gratitude for Slamdance's support, he brought the festival organizers a custom-made 6-inch gummy sign that read "Slamdance," crafted in his factory.

During his time exploring Main Street, David had some interesting experiences. In one western store, the owner, who knew of the legendary tailor Nudie Cohn, noticed David's unique style and pointed out that he was wearing his hat backward. When she realized it was beginning to rain, she insisted he pay $5 for a hat cover to protect it, which David gladly accepted.

Another memorable encounter happened when David saw Robert Redford dining in a nearby restaurant. Though he would have loved to introduce himself, David chose to respect Redford's privacy. Later, David wandered into a candy shop, where the owner asked him about the documentary being shown across the street. When David explained he was the creator of Jelly Belly, the shop owner was skeptical. David offered to buy him a ticket so he could see the documentary for himself. After watching, the owner admitted he had initially believed Marinus Van Dam, a former candy maker at the company, was the true inventor.

This brought back memories of Marinus. Although Marinus was a skilled cook who had worked with David in the early days, his role was limited to following David's instructions and perfecting the recipe. Marinus, however, was proud of his contributions and often claimed he was the creator. David respected his skills and wasn't overly bothered by Marinus's pride, as he knew he was the true inventor of Jelly Belly. When

Marinus passed away on January 6, 1997, *The San Jose Mercury News* ran a headline that read, "Jelly Belly Inventor Dies." This led to some confusion, and one of David's relatives even called his family to ask if David had passed away. But David took it in stride; he appreciated Marinus's skills as a cook, and he respected that Marinus took pride in his work, even if the credit wasn't accurate.

While in Park City, David also met some wonderful people, including a woman from RubySnap Fresh Cookies, a Salt Lake City cookie company. She brought David a box of cookies, and he immediately became a fan. David loves supporting good people, and he highly recommends anyone visiting Salt Lake City to stop by RubySnap and try some of their delicious cookies.

After Slamdance, the documentary continued to attract attention, screening at Hot Docs in Toronto, where David and his son Bert traveled for several press appearances. David participated in interviews with NPR, as well as local radio and TV stations. A coordinator from Slamdance, who had flown in to help him manage his appearances, came down with a sore throat on the day of the first screening. David quickly went to a pharmacy and bought her a pack of Fisherman's Friend lozenges, a childhood remedy known for its awful taste but quick effectiveness. Within ten minutes, her throat felt better, and she was able to introduce him on stage later that night. The topic of the evening was "Random Acts of Kindness," and she shared the story of David's thoughtful gesture with the audience.

On their way back to California, David and Bert arrived at Toronto's airport four hours early and decided to pass the time at a nearby restaurant. David ordered a burger, only to find it rancid, the worst he'd ever tasted. As they left the restaurant, a man noticed David's distinctive hat. "I saw you at Hot Docs and loved your film," he said, introducing himself as James Ackerman, the CEO of The Documentary Channel. Excited, James informed David that his network planned to acquire *Candyman*.

Curious, David asked James why he chose *Candyman* out of the 180 films he had reviewed. James explained that *Candyman* was "number one in the buzz," which meant it had generated the most excitement. During their conversation, David learned that James's father had been an executive producer of *Bewitched* and that his mother had played Betty on *Father Knows Best*. David was impressed by James's confidence in the film, and The Documentary Channel even hired a public relations firm to help promote it. This led to an appearance for David on a morning show in Tampa, Florida, which he and Bert traveled to attend.

The Documentary Channel aired *Candyman: The David Klein Story* on Thanksgiving and Christmas, two of the highest-viewership days of the year. David admired James Ackerman's business acumen, which had turned the channel profitable before it was ultimately sold. Looking back, David realized that even the worst experiences—like a bad burger—could sometimes lead to incredible opportunities.

Through all of this, David has always focused on finding the positives in life's unexpected twists. His setbacks have only deepened his appreciation for the victories that followed. The *Candyman* documentary gave him a platform to finally share his story, and he was grateful for the kindness, support, and unexpected friendships that he encountered along the way.

Brown-Eyed Girl

Stephanie's fascination with adventure began in childhood. Her brown eyes, warm and curious, always sparkled when there was even the hint of a mystery. She loved anything that combined treasure, riddles, and the thrill of discovery. In 2012, that curiosity led her to stumble upon *Candyman: The David Klein Story*, a documentary about David Klein, the original inventor of the Jelly Belly jelly bean. Stephanie watched, captivated by David's innovative spirit and unique way of thinking. His story of creativity and resilience spoke to her on a deep level. She felt a strange but powerful pull to connect with him.

After a few internet searches, she found David's email address. She crafted a message brimming with enthusiasm, pitching a lollipop idea she had been toying with. It would contain a hidden message inside, like a sugary, whimsical cousin of the Magic 8 Ball. She envisioned children marveling at the small secret message inside each candy, like a playful fortune. But in Stephanie's concept, this lollipop would be coated in a layer of candy that would need to be licked away to reveal the message underneath—a surprise waiting for those curious enough to discover it. When David responded, he was thrilled by her idea but realistic about the production challenges. "Stephanie, I love this concept," he wrote, "but the mold alone would cost about $10,000." They exchanged a few emails, shared some laughs, and Stephanie felt a kinship with him, even as life soon took them on separate paths.

Stephanie's life was soon consumed by another treasure—a real one, supposedly hidden in the Rocky Mountains by a millionaire named Forrest Fenn. Fenn had written a memoir filled with tales of his adventures, and, within it, a cryptic poem that hinted at the location of a hidden chest worth a million dollars. Stephanie dove head-first into the search. Her husband's health was uncertain, and, as an agoraphobe, she struggled with the limitations that confined her. But she believed that if she could find Fenn's treasure, it would bring her and her children a new level of security. Her family became her driving force.

In her search for clues, she joined an online community of like-minded adventurers. One day, scrolling through Facebook, Stephanie came across a group run by a toy inventor who had once appeared on *Shark Tank*. The group was lively and engaging, filled with discussions about creative businesses and inventions. To her surprise, David Klein was there too, sprinkling in his own playful questions. "If you could change anything about Tootsie Rolls," he asked, "what would it be?" His posts were fun, insightful, and undeniably popular with the members, especially with Stephanie.

Over the next few weeks, she noticed that while most members enjoyed David's posts, the group's owner grew increasingly frustrated with David's popularity in the group. Finally, the owner told David not to post so much. This bothered David, and he decided to stop altogether. Stephanie and others felt disappointed by his absence. She reached out to David, curious about his sudden silence. David explained the situation, telling her he didn't want to create conflict with the owner. Stephanie encouraged him to start his own group. When he didn't respond, she decided to take matters into her own hands. Within minutes, she created "David Klein's Entrepreneur Group," inviting him and others. The group grew swiftly to over 800 members, each benefiting from David's wisdom and encouragement.

As the group flourished, a high school student named PJ caught everyone's attention. PJ shared David's relentless curiosity about business and ideas. David saw in PJ a younger version of himself, and their bond deepened through their shared love of innovation.

Amidst her treasure hunting, Stephanie's husband made the decision to end their marriage after 27 years together. In the wake of her husband's departure, her father—whom she had lovingly cared for through his battle with Parkinson's—passed away. These hardships weighed heavily on her, but her children kept her grounded and gave her purpose.

During this turbulent time, Stephanie considered a fresh start in Florida. She shared her plans with David, who surprised her by saying that he and Rebecca were also ready for a new beginning. California had grown too costly, and the memories there were taking a toll on him. Moving to Florida sounded like the chance they all needed for a fresh chapter.

In Clearwater, Florida, Stephanie and David found solace in one another's company. They leaned on each other, creating a community within their neighborhood. David, now her close friend and confidant, supported her decision-making and inspired her daily. He'd call anyone, regardless of rank, to resolve an issue or share an idea. She admired his courage and relentless curiosity.

When David opened a candy shop in Clearwater, they met a man named Wes. A candy wholesaler, Wes was passionate about his family and business. David and Stephanie felt an immediate connection with him, especially as Wes's stories reminded them of their own shared history of resilience. Tragically, Wes's life was cut short by Parkinson's, but he left a lasting impression on David and Stephanie.

After one particularly challenging day dealing with difficult clients, Stephanie and David came up with a playful solution to keep their spirits high. They taped a paper plate on the wall, with the heading, "Good People We Know." They started listing the names of people who had shown them kindness, loyalty, and integrity. Wes and PJ topped the list of eight names, and that paper plate became a comforting reminder. Whenever a bad day came along, they'd look at that list, laugh, and remember that there were still good people in the world.

In 2017, Hurricane Irma struck, and the damage forced Stephanie and David to reconsider their lives near the coast. They decided to relocate to Ocala, moving onto a quaint loquat tree farm near a neighborhood called Jumbolair. To their amazement, they discovered that their new neighbor was none other than John Travolta, whose property sat within the gated community across the street.

Through all the ups and downs, Stephanie and David felt more like twinflames with every passing day. They shared an unbreakable bond, bound by a shared love for innovation, adventure, and a refusal to let life's hardships dampen their spirits. Stephanie could always count on David to dream up the next big idea or call someone who could help. David could count on Stephanie to approach each new day with energy and optimism.

One day, as they talked about snack ideas, Stephanie brought up her concerns about peanuts being served on flights. A family member of hers had a peanut allergy, and she found it odd that airlines would serve peanuts thousands of feet in the air, where medical help was hard to reach. David agreed and, without hesitation, picked up the phone and called Southwest Airlines. He told them they should consider offering another snack option and asked the representative if his suggestion would reach someone who could make that decision.

The next month, news broke that Southwest Airlines would be discontinuing peanuts on their flights. Stephanie was grateful and impressed by the impact of David's call. Together, they continued exploring the world around them, celebrating their friendship, and finding joy in the simplest moments.

Their journey reminded them both that, even amidst life's chaos, there were always new adventures waiting to unfold. For Stephanie, the brown-eyed girl, and David, her kindred spirit, life's greatest treasure had been finding each other.

X Marks the Spot

David and Stephanie planned their grand adventure out West, determined to chase the mystery and legend of Forrest Fenn's hidden treasure. Stephanie had been searching for years, and now David was joining her. They embarked on countless trips, trekking through Yellowstone's rugged terrain, navigating Red Rocks' cliffs in Colorado, and searching Santa Fe's hidden nooks, each journey filled with excitement, hope, and occasional missteps. As the trips piled up, even David's wife, Rebecca, joined in, becoming part of the treasure-seeking crew.

Rebecca and Stephanie quickly hit it off, spending hours discussing art and crafting projects during long drives through vast landscapes. Rebecca, a skilled artist, would sketch scenes as they went along, adding splashes of color to their adventures. While Rebecca was completely at ease on these wilderness treks, David was... well, not exactly "outdoorsy." Hiking was a whole new world for him, one where he discovered new muscles he didn't know existed and an appreciation for fresh air. But he was always a willing partner, ready to take on every new trail, climb, or campsite, fueled by the thrill of the hunt.

One memorable afternoon, they were cruising down a winding road in Colorado, windows down to catch the mountain breeze. Suddenly, David's eyes went wide as he spotted three deer lounging in a pasture nearby, only about 50 feet away. With a panicked look, he turned to Stephanie, "Roll up the windows, now!"

Stephanie, puzzled, asked, "Why?"

David pointed out the window. "Do you see them?" he whispered, his tone deadly serious.

Stephanie stifled a laugh. "David, they're deer. They're not coming for us!"

But David wasn't taking any chances. He scrambled to roll up the window, double-checking to make sure it was secure. Stephanie watched, barely able to hold back her laughter, as David, who used to scoff at the outdoors, was suddenly deeply invested in "wildlife safety." Every time they passed an animal, his nervous glances would earn him a good-natured ribbing.

On another trip, they became convinced that the treasure might be stashed at a Girl Scout camp. Of course, they weren't allowed to just waltz in, so they devised a clever—albeit slightly ridiculous—plan: they'd pose as event planners scouting the area for a business retreat. After all, the camp sometimes rented to outside groups, so it wasn't totally far-fetched.

They showed up, ready to deliver their "pitch," and were greeted by a friendly ranger and his young assistant, who looked about sixteen but had an air of authority. The ranger spotted their bags in the back of the vehicle and, assuming they were staying overnight, called out, "Bring your bags!"

Stephanie and David exchanged confused glances knowing Rebecca was back at the hotel taking a nap. How would they get out of this? They complied though, lugging their suitcases with them. They were directed to a rickety ATV, one that had clearly seen better days. The ranger hopped into the passenger seat, while his assistant took the wheel, grinning as if he were about to enter an ATV race. The ride began with a jolt and quickly escalated into a hair-raising thrill ride through the woods, bouncing over rocks, hills and tree roots with reckless abandon.

"Where... are... we... going?" David called out, each word jostled out of him with every bump.

"Just a quick tour!" the assistant yelled back, taking a particularly sharp turn.

David gripped the side of the ATV tightly, his eyes round with alarm. Stephanie, wedged in the back, was being tossed around like popcorn, barely able to decide if she should laugh or cry. It didn't help that the ranger looked suspiciously relaxed, as if he might've had a bit too much "liquid courage" with lunch. And the assistant drove like he was in a backroads rally, determined to get them to their destination in record time.

When they finally reached the cabins, which were bare and rustic, Stephanie noticed a large deer casually grazing in the yard. David muttered something about "dangerous creatures" and sidestepped around it, casting wary glances at the creature. Realizing the treasure wasn't anywhere nearby, David and Stephanie waited for a moment when the ranger and his assistant were distracted, grabbed their bags, and bolted into the woods like fugitives on the run. They made it to the car a mile away, breathless and laughing, convinced that they'd narrowly escaped a wild wilderness plot.

Another memorable misadventure took them far afield, all the way to Indiana. The treasure was supposed to be out West, but every treasure hunter occasionally latches onto an absurd theory. This was one of those times.

It all began at an aquarium in Colorado, where they came across a peculiar gold sluice display that showcased candy gold. Part of Forrest's poem to the treasure seeker included the line, "I give you title to the gold." David, with his vast candy knowledge, had an epiphany: the display was a candy holder, likely from Squire Boone's candy company! And Squire Boone, as luck would have it, had his very own caverns in Indiana.

They set off for the cavern, and when they arrived, they found themselves standing at the entrance of a tour. For David, this was nothing short of a nightmare. He was deathly afraid of heights, and the cavern's metal stairs offered a clear view straight down—at least 50 feet or more. As they descended, he clung to the railing with each step, eyes squeezed shut at the thought of the drop beneath them. Stephanie offered him encouraging words, though she had to hide a smile as the rest of the tour group patiently waited each time he lagged behind. Forret's poem had a line "if your brave and in the wood". It had to be inside the coffin they both thought!

At last, they reached the main attraction: the wooden coffin, supposedly holding none other than Squire Boone himself. David leaned over, glancing left and right to make sure no one was looking. "Alright," he whispered to Stephanie, "as soon as everyone clears out, I'm going over that little wall, and I'm opening it up. Bet the treasure's right in there!"

Stephanie's eyes widened. "David, no! We'll get thrown out!"

David, grinning mischievously, finally relented, though he couldn't shake the idea. As they left the cavern, he was certain he'd come this close to uncovering the prize.

But he wasn't about to give up so easily. The next day, they called their friend Jared to join the search. Jared, who was practically family, was up for the adventure. David came up with a new plan: he'd pretend to be a potential buyer of the caverns. The tour guide, a frail elderly man, was visibly intrigued by David's "interest" in the property, and the trio set off on a private tour.

As they reached the end of the route, Jared struck up a lively conversation with the guide. Then, quick as a flash, David hopped the little wall and tried to lift the coffin's lid. But he was met with the undeniable resistance of screws—Squire Boone's coffin was securely fastened, clearly meant to keep prying hands away.

"What do you think you're doing?" the guide stammered, his face pale with shock.

David shot him a charming smile. "If I'm going to buy the place, I need to make sure Squire's in there, don't I?"

The guide, flustered, sputtered a bit, but before he could say anything, David quickly hopped back over, grinning like a kid who'd just pulled off the ultimate prank. It was an incident they would laugh about for years.

Then came the desert trek.

One scorching 100-degree day, David and Stephanie set out into the desert with a determined plan to reach their next "spot"—an area they were convinced held the treasure. As they trudged through the blistering heat, it became clear that David was struggling. He had slowed to a shuffle, beads of sweat glistening on his forehead as he tried to keep up with Stephanie's steady pace.

Finally, Stephanie, noticing the toll the heat was taking on David, paused and spotted a lone sliver of shade—a skinny electric pole casting a tiny bit of respite from the blazing sun. She pointed to it and said, "David, please sit here. I'll go the rest of the way and check it out."

David didn't argue. With a sigh of relief, he sank down, letting the thin shadow cover his face. "Be careful," he called, though his voice was barely more than a croak.

Stephanie trekked on, crossing two more grueling miles to reach their spot, heart pounding as she scanned the ground for any signs of a treasure. But after what felt like an eternity of searching, she came up empty-handed. She let out a disappointed sigh and turned back to retrace her steps, ready to tell David the disappointing news.

When she returned, she found David looking decidedly unsettled. His face was a mixture of disbelief and horror, his gaze darting left and right. She approached, confused.

"Are you alright?" she asked, trying not to laugh.

David nodded stiffly, his eyes fixed on something behind her. "The whole time you were gone... there were these... things... watching me," he muttered, looking genuinely rattled.

Stephanie turned to see a small army of prairie dogs popping up and down all around him, their little faces peeking out of burrows as if judging this strange intruder in their land. She couldn't help herself and burst into laughter, realizing that David, who already wasn't much for nature, had spent the past half-hour convinced he was about to be eaten alive by prairie dogs.

They shared a laugh and started the trek back to the car, Stephanie giggling as David shot wary glances at the critters until they reached the safety of the vehicle. But just five minutes down the road, as they drove, they saw something that stopped them in their tracks. A break in the fence—one that led directly to the very spot they'd spent hours hiking to reach. They could have simply parked, strolled right in, and avoided the whole ordeal.

The absurdity of it hit them both at once. They laughed so hard they could barely catch their breath, each chuckle laced with the absurdity of their entire desert misadventure.

But their travels weren't always so amusing. One day, they found themselves in a very different situation in Raton, New Mexico. As they drove along a deserted park trail, the car suddenly lurched and got stuck in deep muddy sand, miles from the nearest paved road. They barely had cell service, but Stephanie managed to reach AAA, only to be told, "Sorry, no coverage if you're on a dirt road." They did manage to call a tow company, though, and were assured someone would be there soon. Hoping they were able to describe where they actually were to the driver.

After three sweltering hours in the sun, though, they were still waiting. David looked around the car, his eyes landing on a half-empty bottle of water in the cup holder. The blazing heat was starting to wear them down, and David, ever the gentleman, picked up the bottle and handed it to Stephanie. "That's yours," he said solemnly, "take it."

Stephanie looked at him, eyes glistening with gratitude. "You are amazing," she whispered. You're willing to give me the last drop of water?

Then, glancing into the back seat, she pointed to the case of water bottles resting there. David's expression shifted from noble to relief as they both burst into laughter, the tension broken.

After what felt like ages, a man and his young son appeared in a pickup just by chance meeting, and willing to help. The man, with no hesitation, crawled under their car getting mud all over himself, connecting it to the tow line as his son watched closely, learning the ropes from his dad. They were free! David and Stephanie thanked them profusely, offering a reward, which the man politely declined. But they made sure to tell his son what a good person his father was, hoping it'd leave a lasting impression.

Finally back on solid ground, they waved goodbye, grateful not only for the rescue but for the kindness they'd encountered that day. On occasion when David and Stephanie find themselves on some sandy road, David can be heard quietly whispering, Raton.

Some moments were peaceful, like watching the sunrise over Colorado Springs at the Garden of the Gods, or the time they drove through Yellowstone and found themselves face-to-face with a lone bison with no one else around, just them and nature.

They'd sit quietly, imagining the lives of early pioneers, marveling at the beauty of the land from an old abandoned house.

Of course, not every local was as friendly. Once, while exploring San Lazaro, New Mexico—home to a property Forrest Fenn himself had owned—they encountered a less-than-welcoming neighbor. "Turn around," he growled. "Or I've got a gun, and I'm not afraid to use it."

Without a word, David whipped the car around and they sped off, laughing nervously. It became an inside joke; anytime they passed an isolated house, David would mutter, "Hope they don't have a gun."

Finally, they learned that the Forrest Fenn treasure was said to be found by a man named Jack. But whether it was true or not, they had already found their real treasure: a journey filled with unforgettable adventures, friendship, and enough stories to last a lifetime.

Candy Thinking and a Good Friend

Rich

The story of David Klein and his journey through the candy industry begins like a tale woven with sweet serendipity, friendships, and hard business lessons. Among the most treasured friendships of his life was the one he shared with Rich, a sales manager at the Herman Goelitz Candy Company—the company that brought David's Jelly Belly Jelly Beans to life. Rich wasn't just a business associate; he was a close friend who stood by David through years of ups and downs, of ideas that stuck and others that slipped away like grains of sugar through fingertips.

Their friendship blossomed in the early days of Jelly Belly's inception. David still remembers the day the phrase "The Original Gourmet Jelly Bean" was coined. For years, Rich playfully claimed that the words were his own. David had always laughed it off, letting Rich take credit in their friendly banter. But now, with decades of perspective, David can finally say with conviction, "Yes, Rich, it was you." It was a line that encapsulated the essence of what Jelly Belly would come to mean—a candy made with care, one that set itself apart as something special in a world full of sweets.

Rich was more than a friend; he was a craftsman in his own right, a perfectionist who ensured that each candy he presented was nothing short of perfect. David admired this about him, especially when Rich would passionately describe new creations from the Herman Goelitz factory. Each candy was a story in itself, detailed meticulously by Rich in ways that would make anyone's mouth water.

Eventually, Rich moved on from Herman Goelitz, taking his dedication and passion for candy creation with him. He and the highly skilled candy maker, Marinus began a new venture, building a factory from scratch and crafting treats that sparkled with Rich's perfectionism and Marinus's craftsmanship. In the early days of their production, Rich flew to Burbank, California, to show David their new lineup, his pride almost palpable as he laid out samples of what they'd created. David couldn't help but be impressed. Among all the candies, David had one particular idea in mind—a twist on a classic treat. He asked Rich, "Could you make a cookies and cream malt ball?" David envisioned using Oreo Mint Cookies and classic Oreo Cookies for two varieties, a treat that would taste like pure nostalgia.

Rich's eyes lit up at the suggestion, and he immediately agreed. David proposed becoming a distributor for the product, settling on a modest profit of 17 cents for every pound produced. The first batch was a hit, and every month, without fail, David received a check from the factory, signed by Marinus himself. For two years, this arrangement thrived, until one day when Rich left the company, the checks stopped arriving.

When two months passed without a word, David reached out to Marinus, hoping for some explanation. Calmly, he asked, "What happened to the royalty checks?" Marinus's response was curt, almost dismissive, "There won't be any more checks. Your deal was with Rich, not with me." Stunned, David reminded him, "But you are the one who signed the checks." Marinus's voice was cold as stone. "I don't care," he said, before ending the conversation. David never spoke to Marinus again, and to this day, the cookies and cream malt balls continue to appear on candy shelves everywhere, a silent reminder of a deal that was as sweet as it was bittersweet.

Not every experience was quite so heartbreaking, though. Some brought unexpected excitement and inspiration. David's passion for innovation never dimmed, especially when it came to Jelly Beans. It was in the late 1980s when David had another brainstorm—a new candy he called "Peek-a-boos," a miniature chocolate nonpareil that he thought would charm fans everywhere. The idea was simple yet brilliant, and David began shipping these treats from Baker Chocolate to the Herman Goelitz's major locations in Oakland and North Chicago as Herm the owner wanted to be the distributor. It was a humble arrangement; David earned a small profit, enough to keep him satisfied as Peek-a-boos began flying off shelves.

Then, one day, the orders stopped. David soon learned the hard truth: Herman Goelitz had gone behind his back, placing their own order directly with the manufacturer. They even changed the name to "Dimples," effectively cutting him out of the equation.

In 2016, as David was closing his California factory to start fresh in Florida, an afternoon conversation with his friend Stephanie sparked yet another idea. They were talking about their love for Jelly Beans, and the conversation meandered toward Stephanie's favorite beverage: chai tea. The smell of coffee and chai, she told him, was her personal favorite. "Why not a line of coffee-inspired Jelly Beans?" David thought aloud, his mind racing with possibilities.

Stephanie was as thrilled as he was. They brainstormed flavors that would capture the essence of a coffeehouse: Macchiato, Chai Tea, Coffee and Donuts, Double Buzz (for an extra kick of caffeine), and Hot Cocoa with peppermint. David knew he needed a partner to bring these beans to life, so he connected with Curtis at Mount Franklin's candy division, Sunrise. Curtis was equally excited and spent months working with David on crafting these special beans, which David would then finish at his factory with a final layer of flavor.

To fund their venture, they launched a Kickstarter, and with Stephanie's family handling the campaign, the support rolled in. The project reached its goal in no time, creating a buzz in the candy world. Soon, even large chains like Starbucks and Cracker Barrel were expressing interest in the Coffee House Beans. When it came time to fulfill the Kickstarter orders, Stephanie flew to California, and together, they filled every box with beans, fueled by the excitement of their shared creation.

David's friend, Ed, was among the first to taste the Coffee House Beans, devouring handfuls with unabashed enthusiasm. "You shouldn't mix the flavors!" David laughed, watching Ed enjoy each chaotic handful. But Ed couldn't resist—they were that good.

Then, just as momentum was building, they hit a wall. David placed a $4,000 order with Curtis at Sunrise, but the next day, Curtis called with disappointing news. The owner had decided against doing business with anyone running a Kickstarter campaign. It was as if all their dreams had been dashed with a single phone call. David and Stephanie couldn't make sense of it. How could a company turn down an order just because of their funding source? They were certain that a competitor had intervened, sensing David's return to the jelly bean market and moving to stifle his success.

And so, David's journey through the world of candy continued, filled with as many twists and turns as the flavors he dreamed up. From friendships forged in sugar to bitter betrayals, every chapter was a reminder that sweetness and struggle were often two sides of the same coin.

If you've ever felt wronged and wanted to take a stand against injustice, please consider buying a book for a friend or two to support David's mission to pay off this billion-dollar company and gain financial freedom from the brand that owns the jelly bean he invented. Your support could make a meaningful impact. And if you have ideas on how to help, David would be grateful to welcome you into his family of supporters. Thank you for standing with him!

The Gold Ticket

David and Stephanie's leap into treasure hunting began with a spark of frustration. They had eagerly joined the famous Forrest Fenn treasure hunt, like so many others, but something about it didn't feel right, especially to Stephanie. The hunt seemed to favor a select few, which didn't seem fair. Disappointed, they wondered, "Why not create a treasure hunt of our own?"—one that would welcome everyone equally. They envisioned something that would be both challenging and inclusive, giving people from all walks of life a fair shot at the thrill of discovery.

Their idea quickly grew into an ambitious plan: a treasure hunt spanning nine states, with each location carefully chosen not only for its beauty but also for a touch of historical significance or personal meaning. Stephanie took charge of creating the riddles, crafting them to be tricky yet solvable. They would be challenging enough to keep participants hooked. The treasure? Simple yet meaningful: a gold colored dog tag stamped with a unique code, symbolizing both the journey and the reward.

Every trip to hide the tags became a significant moment for Stephanie. Living with agoraphobia, she didn't travel alone, but sitting in the driver's seat with David by her side gave her comfort and confidence. David, always supportive, embraced her quirks and encouraged her along the way. He even came up with his own quirky method for choosing their hiding spots, often typing random weather queries into Google in order to know what city they were in and letting fate guide them to unexpected destinations. This serendipitous approach led them to Jellico, Tennessee. Jellico was a small town with a poignant story that left a deep impression on both of them.

Jellico's story dated back to 1944, when a train full of young soldiers tragically derailed there and 33 men died and hundreds were injured. Learning about it touched both David and Stephanie deeply, reminding them of the sacrifices and stories often hidden in small towns. They felt the weight of the past and saw how they could honor such stories in their treasure hunt, weaving local history into their clues. For David and Stephanie, the hunt was about more than just hidden dog tags; it was a way of connecting people to places and stories, making each location feel like more than just a point on a map.

One of their early stops was with their friend Mindy Fausey, a fellow treasure hunter they'd met during a Forrest Fenn gathering in New Mexico. Mindy and her partner James had just settled into a beautiful mountaintop home in Virginia, complete with its own waterfall and sweeping views. Standing there with Mindy, sharing their plans for the hunt, they felt a renewed excitement as she encouraged them. Mindy's enthusiasm only solidified their resolve. Mindy traveled with them to look for another treasure that was said to be hidden in North Carolina. Though they didn't uncover any other treasures that day, they did find the perfect place to stash one of their gold tags. With Mindy joining their small team, they had an ally they could count on to help manage the hunt's many moving pieces.

Back in Florida, David's vision for the treasure hunt only grew. After a call with an old journalist friend from the Associated Press, he got an idea. The friend had remarked that the story wasn't newsworthy for his publication because it only covered a few states. Inspired, David told Stephanie, "Why not make this nationwide?" Their plan quickly evolved from nine states to all fifty, and to make it even more exciting, he decided to offer the candy factory as the grand prize. Stephanie thought he was a bit crazy, but his enthusiasm was infectious, and soon they were planning a treasure hunt that would span the entire country. Each state's winner would receive $5,000, and everyone would have a shot at winning the candy factory itself.

News about the hunt spread like wildfire. Almost overnight, their inbox filled with messages from people whose lives had been touched by the idea. One woman shared how she'd always dreamed of finding a golden ticket with her grandfather, while another woman grieving the loss of her brother and son saw the hunt as a chance to reconnect with her family. A man recovering from a heart attack wrote to tell them that the treasure hunt had brought him joy for the first time since his medical struggle. Each story reminded David and Stephanie of why they'd embarked on this wild journey in the first place.

The morning after the hunt went viral, Stephanie shared the exciting news with her longtime friend, Forrest Fenn. They had a quick, cheerful conversation, but little did Stephanie know, it would be their last. Forrest passed away the very next day, leaving her with a profound sense of loss. Her uncle had always loved the word "synchronicity," and it seemed fitting here. She couldn't shake the feeling that she was meant to have that final conversation with Forrest, the man whose own treasure hunt had inspired her and David, one last time.

Stephanie and David

With the growing interest came logistical challenges. Their website struggled under the influx of visitors, crashing frequently. Desperate for a solution, David reached out to a professor he knew, who connected him to a business manager they'd later call "Mr. Badman." For a hefty fee, Mr. Badman promised to rebuild the site, but instead of solving their issues, his efforts created even more obstacles. He tried to impose a new system that complicated things for Stephanie's small, dedicated team. To make matters worse, Mr. Badman had a hard time taking direction from Stephanie, particularly as a woman, and often dismissed her requests or stalled when she asked him to handle critical issues. Matters came to a head when he locked her out of her own website, refusing to grant access. For hours, Stephanie and her team were shut out of the site, and she experienced what she later described as one of the biggest panic attacks of her life. Finally, David managed to ease Mr. Badman's ego, and once they regained control of the site, they promptly let him go.

After Mr. Badman's departure, the "homespun" team stepped in to keep things running smoothly. Stephanie's daughter, Ashley; her nephews, Kyle and Kory; her friend Mindy; and Ed, a friend in Bosnia, all took on various roles, learning the ropes as they went. Despite the initial challenges, they managed to get the site back up and running, each person bringing their unique skills to the table and working tirelessly to support the treasure hunt's success. Mindy's children helped and Keith, a good friend jumped in to help with the facebook page.

Despite these obstacles, David and Stephanie pressed on. They scheduled treasure hunts every weekend and even adjusted the calendar to avoid overlapping hunts in neighboring states. Yet, surprises kept coming. The first hunt launched in Georgia, where the gold ticket was hidden beneath a sprawling Magnolia tree, deep within thick brush. The placement was deliberate, meant to be challenging even for those who knew the location. But soon after the Georgia hunt began, an unexpected buzz hit the Gold Ticket Facebook page: someone had already found the gold ticket. It seemed impossible. The riddle hadn't even been released, and yet somehow, this participant had ventured into the brush and located it. Suspicion arose when the person, a woman from Georgia, began asking if anyone had a spare ticket for the already sold-out Georgia hunt. When David managed to call her, she confirmed she had indeed found the gold ticket.

After a tense discussion, David and Stephanie decided not to withhold the prize money from the early finder, even though their terms allowed for it. "It's a PR nightmare waiting to happen," David reasoned. Paying her would set the right tone for the treasure hunt, fostering good faith among participants. In the end, they agreed it was the best choice. On their YouTube channel, David and Stephanie explained the situation to the players, who responded with a mix of admiration and frustration. Some were impressed with the integrity of the decision, while others felt shortchanged, demanding refunds. Thankfully, the latter were few, and David and Stephanie were able to move forward, re-hiding a new ticket in Georgia and ensuring the adventure continued.

When a riddle was released for their treasure hunt, David and Stephanie would watch the clock intently, silently hoping it wouldn't be solved immediately. Many dedicated treasure hunters staked out locations across their state, waiting in spots they suspected it might be. Some families went as far as positioning multiple members in different places, ready to pounce on the solution. As the minutes ticked by, David and Stephanie would quietly cheer each milestone. After 15 minutes, they'd exchange glances and say it aloud, and when 30 minutes passed, they'd sigh with relief. But it was only after a full hour that they'd really start to relax, grateful that the hunt was lasting long enough to keep everyone engaged, excited, and not disappointed.

Throughout the Gold Ticket journey, unexpected obstacles popped up. In one instance, a ticket was found cemented in place after being hidden under a statue due to a city's concern over the removal of certain statues. When a ticket became inaccessible, the first person to submit the correct location was awarded the prize as the "solver." In another case, the hunt in Virginia nearly spiraled out of control when a ticket was hidden on private museum grounds. Eager treasure hunters descended in droves, riling the property owner, who called David in a fury as a crowd gathered to dig through wood chips. The police were called to manage the situation, and even the local news arrived to cover the unusual scene. To smooth things over, David sent the owner $500, hoping to ease the tension and keep the hunt on track.

Then came a particularly tricky incident in West Virginia. One participant claimed to have found the correct location and, determined to prove it, drove to the spot at 5 a.m., capturing video to send to David and Stephanie as evidence that the ticket was no longer there. The video, along with the fact that the park had been manicured since the ticket's hiding, convinced David and Stephanie that the claim was legitimate. They awarded $5,000 to this participant and, upon reviewing their records, discovered that another person had also submitted the correct location before this. To maintain fairness, they awarded that person as well, bringing the total to $10,000. To further restore trust among the players, they chose to run a new West Virginia hunt with a fresh prize, which another lucky winner claimed, receiving $5,000.

About a month after this incident, Stephanie and David were stunned to receive an email with a photo of the original West Virginia gold ticket. A mother and son had discovered it, their story unfolding with an unusual twist—the son's father worked for a company that managed city park maintenance, sparking questions about whether it was mere coincidence or something more. To keep peace, they also were given $5,000.

The North Dakota hunt also faced a sudden roadblock when David received an urgent call from the attorney general's office, effectively shutting them down. The office deemed the hunt a potential legal issue, as it hadn't been cleared by the state. After a series of phone calls and pleas, David managed to make his case, arguing that the treasure hunt was a skill-based competition, not unlike a spelling bee or a little league game. The attorney general's office couldn't dispute this reasoning and, just hours before the scheduled release of the riddle, gave them the green light.

Those few months of the Gold Ticket hunt were riddled with challenges and surprises. Yet, in the midst of these unexpected turns, it was a time of pure adventure, uniting strangers in pursuit of a shared, golden goal.

As the hunts unfolded across the country, each state brought unforgettable stories. In Tennessee, the winner's screams of excitement were captured on video and was shared with all the searchers to see a LIVE treasure hunt find. Then, in New York, a young woman was out searching with her mother, who was on the phone with her husband—a prominent New York attorney. Unbeknownst to them, he was using a dictation device during the call, and the entire discovery was recorded, capturing the family's surprise and joy. Days later, they discovered the recording and realized they had preserved that moment forever. It was these kinds of unexpected memories that added magic to David and Stephanie's hunt.

Over time, the community around the hunt became as memorable as the adventures themselves. There were two military women who dubbed themselves "Team Second Place" after they came close to victory multiple times. Then there was "Hippy Dude," whose videos and humorous commentary entertained countless searchers, and others who made a name for themselves with creative approaches and quirky personalities. A man named Doug created giant gold tickets for players that were so cool. There were two sets of twin ladies who created fun videos that were shared on facebook and no one can forget Katrina and her crew of littles. Katrina would single handedly take her children out for adventure after adventure displaying photos online of their orderly chairs and meals all in a row while looking over a beautiful view.

Jason's discovery of the gold ticket in Anniston, Alabama, became one of the most memorable moments of David and Stephanie's treasure hunt. They had stumbled upon a quiet alley with a striking mural of a life-sized bus painted along the wall. Initially, the scene held no particular meaning, until they spotted a small post with a button attached. Curious, they pressed it, and immediately, the voices of the Freedom Riders filled the alley, recounting the harrowing events of May 14, 1961. Tears streamed down Stephanie's face as the powerful stories echoed, and they knew in that instant this was the right spot. But hiding a gold ticket here proved tricky; the alley seemed bare, with nowhere to conceal it—except for one solitary door across from the mural. At the bottom of this door, they noticed a small threshold with a hollow channel, just big enough to slip the gold ticket inside.

Jason found that ticket, and through him, David and Stephanie got to know his family. They met his mother, whom he often brought along on treasure trips, and his children and wife, who later treated them to the best apple cake they'd ever tasted.

But as the hunt gained popularity, a situation arouse. The trouble stemmed from an unexpected source, the Jelly Belly Candy Company. Without warning, the company issued a "correction" minimizing David's role in their history, describing him as merely the creator of the name and subtly implying that he had little to do with the candy itself. The carefully worded statement painted David as a scammer and damaged his reputation. It was a painful blow, but David and Stephanie stayed afloat thanks to the unwavering support of most of their treasure hunting community.

Despite the setbacks, David and Stephanie were reminded of the happiness they'd brought to people's lives. One treasure hunter even told them that, thanks to the hunt, she had met her future husband. Another said it saved her marriage. These stories were the fuel that kept them going. Though the hunt eventually came to a close, the memories remained with David and Stephanie. They had brought joy, adventure, and a bit of magic to countless lives, and they hoped to one day revive the gold ticket hunt with their beloved four-line riddles. For now, though, they looked back on it as a wild, unforgettable chapter during the trying time of Covid. It brought hope and joy during such terrible times. A chapter they will treasure forever, full of people who started as strangers and became family along the way.

Lawsuits

David Klein poured his heart and soul into Jelly Belly. He was the visionary who created the brand, investing years of hard work, creativity, and relentless dedication. David appeared on over 100 radio, TV shows and publications. There would be no Jelly Belly if he hadn't invented it. After selling his interest in Jelly Belly, David wanted to move forward and create new successes. Yet, he found himself feeling misrepresented. The Jelly Belly Candy Company portrayed him as if he were a truck driver who had stumbled upon a catchy name, completely ignoring his true role in creating Jelly Belly's success. Their statements made him look like an impostor.

David's efforts had laid the foundation of worldwide success for Jelly Belly, but this dedication came at a personal cost, keeping him from spending time with his young family. His endless hours of work and devotion had given Jelly Belly the momentum to grow, and anyone could have taken it further once he'd built that worldwide success. Herman Goelitz was at maximum capacity when David lost his Jelly Bellies. When he hired Herman Goelitz's company to become his contract manufacturer/copacker, he never imagined his own role would be so diminished in its history. They were a small little company that had to run to the post office to see if there were any checks in the mail to cover their payroll. Over time, it seemed Herman Goelitz Candy Company wanted not only to own David's product but to recreate history, making it seem as though they had created it. David wondered: does Yum! Brands still show The Colonel as the founder on KFC? Does Clorox still let everyone know it was Burt who founded Burt's Bees? Is Famous Amos still given his history? Are you, the reader allowed to give your resume out or tell people who your children are? David feels people should be allowed to know what he has accomplished.

During a conversation about an unrelated matter, David shared his frustrations with an attorney. After hearing David's story, the attorney assured him he had a strong case and suggested he should consider filing a lawsuit. So many articles about The Gold Ticket had a "correction" that made David look as if he were a liar. The correction was worded in a misleading manner that unfairly implied David Klein had made a false claim. In reality, David Klein never stated that he was the founder of The Jelly Belly Candy Company that originated from Herm Rowland's operation. He was the founder of his own company, also called The Jelly Belly, which created and launched the original Jelly Belly jelly beans. The correction's phrasing misrepresented Klein's actual statements and made him appear dishonest, despite the fact that he never claimed to have founded Herm Rowland's company. David was hesitant—what he truly wanted was for The Jelly Belly Candy Company to stop making statements that painted him as a liar and simply leave him alone. They could have easily stated, "David Klein is no longer associated with The Jelly Belly," but instead, they would say, "David Klein is not associated with The Jelly Belly," making it look as if he never was. David wanted people to know the truth about his role in Jelly Belly's history, and he hoped journalists would help tell his story accurately in the future to set the record straight.

Deciding he deserved a chance to reclaim his reputation, David agreed to move forward with the lawsuit, as long as he wouldn't be responsible for attorney fees if things went South. Unfortunately, his lawyer, lacked the necessary experience and made crucial errors that derailed the case. These mistakes resulted in The Jelly Belly Candy Company winning a judgement — not because David didn't make a case, but due to some legal failings. David was never given his day in court in front of a jury, yet he was still ordered to pay The Jelly Belly Candy Company an astonishing $276,408.92 in attorney fees.

Just when hope seemed lost, David found an attorney that would help him navigate out of this legal nightmare.

To make matters worse, The Jelly Belly Candy Company filed a lawsuit against David, seeking a declaratory judgment. They wanted a court ruling that would prevent David from claiming he founded The Jelly Belly Candy Company. Though David had NEVER claimed he founded THEIR current company. But with The Herman Goelitz Company having changed their name to The Jelly Belly Candy Company in the year 2000, David was likely to be restricted from ever saying he'd founded a company called "Jelly Belly." David has said he will agree to no longer say that he founded his company The Jelly Belly which was a candy company and he of course will never say he founded their company, but he definitely believes he should have the right to say he was the inventor of The Jelly Belly Jelly Bean. This case ended in a judgement where David has agreed to never say he founded The Jelly Belly Candy Company.

The toll of these legal battles weighed heavily on David and Stephanie too. They stopped posting on social media for their Gold Ticket treasure hunt, fearing Jelly

Belly's watchful eyes would cause them more trouble. What had once been a joyful venture with loyal treasure hunting fans and friends now felt overshadowed by a company determined to control every word they spoke and use it in court.

Adding insult to injury, even after Herman Goelitz sold The Jelly Belly Candy Company to Ferrera in October of 2023, the new owners wanted to block payments to David's new attorney. David had hoped that with the new ownership, he might have a good relationship with the company and maybe even serve as an ambassador for the brand he created, finally feeling a sense of pride once again in Jelly Belly. But the reality was far from what he had imagined.

But David refused to give up. He began writing a tell the truth book, not only to share his side of the story but also to earn the money from book sales to gain some financial freedom and pay off this billion dollar company while he still has time to create the next best thing. Born in 1946, David knows that each opportunity to create is precious, and he wants to help others see the truth, learn from his hardships, and find hope even when things look bleak. He still has a passion for business, ideas, and helping other entrepreneurs get their start. At 78 years old, David hasn't stopped believing in new dreams of success.

David Klein's journey with Jelly Belly is about far more than candy—it's about resilience, fighting for his story, and refusing to be erased.

Dear Friends,

Thank you for going on this journey with me to find out more about who I am and what brought me to this place. I realize that many people in this world have been wronged in life, and I want to show others that there is always hope, always a way to find your way out of a mess—just like I'm trying to do. I also hope that those who have wronged others can find it in themselves to swallow their pride and turn things around. It's never too late to right a wrong.

I appreciate every one of you. Let's make every day a great day.

Warmly,
David.

www.ingramcontent.com/pod-product-compliance
Lightning Source LLC
Chambersburg PA
CBHW061657120626
46550CB00003B/986